Beowulf

EDITED BY M.A. ROBERTS

PRESTWICK HOUSE
LITERARY TOUCHSTONE CLASSICS

P.O. BOX 658 • CLAYTON, DELAWARE 19938

SENIOR EDITOR: Paul Moliken

EDITOR: M.A. Roberts

COVER: Photography by Larry Knox. Beowulf portrayed by Jack Knox.
The Great Sword from the Days of Giants provided by Actors Attic
of Dover, Delaware (www.actorsattic.com).

PRODUCTION: Jerry Clark

PRESTWICK HOUSE
LITERARY TOUCHSTONE CLASSICS

P.O. BOX 658 • CLAYTON, DELAWARE 19938
TEL: 1.800.932.4593
FAX: 1.888.718.9333
WEB: www.prestwickhouse.com

ISBN 978-1-58049-348-2

Beowulf

CONTENTS

NOTES

What is a literary classic and why are these classic works important to the world?

A literary classic is a work of the highest excellence that has something important to say about life and/or the human condition and says it with great artistry. A classic, through its enduring presence, has withstood the test of time and is not bound by time, place, or customs. It speaks to us today as forcefully as it spoke to people one hundred or more years ago, and as forcefully as it will speak to people of future generations. For this reason, a classic is said to have universality.

The epic poem *Beowulf* was written in Old English, also called Anglo-Saxon, the language spoken on the island of Great Britain after the arrival of the Angles and Saxons around 500 A.D. Their language survived and evolved until the Normans conquered the island in 1066.

The author of *Beowulf* is unknown, as is the date of its original composition—although some suppose that the saga was written sometime in the 7th or 8th century. Numerous recitations likely embellished the story and its characters with fantastic elements and exaggerated character traits, including godlike wisdom, intelligence, and nearly superhuman strength and abilities. The poem was most assuredly part of the previous oral tradition of story telling.

Beowulf exists in its present form through one manuscript only, which was penned in the 10th or early 11th century, and it barely escaped a fire in 1731 at the Ashburnham House in Westminster, England.

The first translation did not appear until 1815, and even at that date, it was written in Latin. *Beowulf* was not commonly included in English literature courses until the middle part of the 20th century, after acclaimed author and linguistics professor J.R.R. Tolkien published an essay titled "Beowulf: The Monsters and the Critics." This essay posited that Beowulf was a work of poetic literature, rather than merely an historic document.

This prose edition of *Beowulf* has combined and reconciled the 1892 prose translation by John Earle with the 1910 verse translation by Francis Gummere. These two translations differ considerably from one another textually, although the style and plot lines are similar. When the two translations varied a great deal, we consulted other texts to arrive at a satisfactory resolution of the discrepancies.

For example, Earle's prose version begins:

> *"What ho! we have heard tell of the grandeur of the imperial kings of the spear-bearing Danes in former days, how those ethelings promoted bravery."*

Gummere begins his verse translation:

> *"LO, praise of the prowess of people-kings*
> *of spear-armed Danes, in days long sped,*
> *we have heard, and what honor the athelings*
> *won!"*

Ethelings or *athelings* directly translates as *sons of kings*

The Prestwick House prose version combines the better parts of both texts, changing a few words and reading:

> *"Hark! We have heard of the glory of the kings of men among the spear-bearing Danes in days of long ago. We have heard how the princes won renown!"*

We have made every effort to ensure that the text is readable and still retains the essence of both translations.

When a segment of text is surrounded by brackets, it indicates that a section of the original manuscript has been badly damaged or corrupted, possibly due to the 1731 fire. Chapters XXIX and XXX fall into this category. Prestwick House has followed the Gummere translation, which eliminated both chapters. Other translators have approximated the meanings of some passages, but the actual wording is not at all certain.

Reading Pointers for Sharper Insight

1. *Beowulf*, like almost all Anglo-Saxon poetry, is written with a great deal of alliteration. Alliteration occurs when two or more words in close proximity to one another begin with the same consonant sound. As an example of alliteration, examine the following phrase from our prose rendition:

   > "A foundling was he when he first lay friendless; fate later brought him solace as he waxed in power and flourished in wealth, until folk who lodge on the whale-paths near and far heeded his decree and gave him tribute—that was a good king!"

   The consonant *f* sound is repeated numerous times [*foundling, first, friendless, fate, flourished, folk,* and *far*]. The *w* sound of *was, when, waxed, wealth,* and *whale* is another example of the poem's alliteration.

   The alliterative verse structure in the original Anglo-Saxon follows several rules dealing with which words could and should alliterate. A pause, or *cæsura*, was inserted in the middle of each line of poetry, dividing the line into two parts. The words that were most strongly pronounced or given emphasis in the line were usually the alliterated words. The Prestwick House Literary Touchstone Classic™ rendition of *Beowulf* is in prose and does not follow this specific Anglo-Saxon structure. In all other aspects, however, we have remained faithful to commonly accepted translations.

   • The Anglo-Saxon language of *Beowulf* is filled with compound words called *kennings*, which, in modern terms, are similar to *euphemisms*, or *periphrases*. For example, the term *whale-paths* indicates the oceans, *wave-rider* is a boat or ship, *ring-giver, folk-friend,* or *friend to the people* stands for a king, and a *word-hoard* simply means a vocabulary. This usage is evocative of the subject as the writer conceived it—in this way, kennings often indicate an opinion *about* a noun as well as identifying it. A king, for instance, is one who gives objects of worth or treasure to his supporters; this is the role that the author indicates a king should fulfill. Through the Old English kennings, the idea that the word represents became the word itself. In addition, kennings, because of their multi-syllabic nature, allowed poets to choose phrases that would best fit the verse structure of the poem.

- At many points in the narrative, the characters are not referred to by name. Hrothgar, for instance, is identified as the *white-haired one, a venerable king, a mighty ring-giver,* and so forth. The term *ring-giver* refers to the custom of a king taking golden jewelry he is wearing and bestowing it upon worthy heroes and liegemen.

- Characters are also referenced by their family relations. Here is a list of common terms for the book's characters:

      Hrothgar:
            shield of the Danes/of the people
            helmet/crown of the Danes
            friend of the Scyldings
            son of Healfdene
            chief of Ing's descendants
            lord of the Ingwines
            white-haired
            gold-friend of men

      Beowulf
            son of Ecgtheow
            ring-giver (later in the book, when he returns home and becomes king)

      Unferth
            Hrothgar's orator
            Ecglaf's son/son of Ecglaf

- There are also several points in the saga where the plot digresses, and the narrative tells the story of other legendary people. During various feasts in Heorot (the massive gathering hall of the Danish people), a bard or minstrel breaks into song and tells the tale of another king or hero from Scandinavian lore. Each miniature tale corresponds or contrasts in some way to the characters in the larger saga. Beowulf, for example, is contrasted to Heremod: Beowulf is generous and brave, but Heremod is portrayed as mean-spirited and cowardly. These other tales serve to highlight the character traits of the main heroes of the saga.

- *Beowulf* includes many juxtapositions of pagan and Christian references. The names of the heathen gods have been omitted from the poem itself, but there are still many references to *Fate (Wyrd)* or *destiny,* and the author seems to simultaneously extol both the pursuit of worldly fame and the reliance upon Providence/God. Note that the figure of a boar, which is often mentioned as being mounted on warriors' helmets for protection, is a symbol of *Freyr,* a Germanic god. Freyr is never mentioned by name; however, at other points in the narrative, the author condemns heathen worship.

  It is quite likely—albeit impossible to confirm—that the *Beowulf* we now read is altered somewhat from the version known to early Anglo-Saxons. The saga comes from a time when Anglo-Saxon society was in transition from polytheistic pagan religions to Christianity. Numerous references throughout the poem are attributable to Christian beliefs, but others are obviously not. As an example, after his death, no mention is made of Beowulf's entering heaven; he is, in fact, burned on his funeral pyre, a distinctly pagan ritual. Grendel, even though depicted as an inhuman monster, is frequently equated with Cain, the son of Adam.

- Note the following values of Anglo-Saxon society that are exhibited in *Beowulf*:

  Fame and renown among those who are alive is paramount. Fame is primarily achieved through victorious combat and heroic deeds, which will be turned into a tale that will survive one's death. The final lines of the epic praise Beowulf's virtues, especially that he was *lof-geornost,* or *the most eager for fame.*

  The king, or chieftain, is the *shield, shelterer,* and *protector* of the people: He would give up his life for his people. Good kings and chieftains should be generous with their wealth and richly reward those who serve them well. Weak or bad kings, however, would hoard their wealth, not reward their liegemen, and be cruel or unjust—they do not care for or about their people. A group without a king is vulnerable and weak—the lives of individuals in a leaderless group are filled with sorrow, as other tribes can attack them and cause devastation.

Bravery in battle is a sign of loyalty to a lord because this gains fame, honor, and treasure for him. It is extremely important to be loyal to one's ruler, family, and clan. Good subjects, thanes, and vassals fight for their lord; bad ones will shrink in fear when combat comes.

PRELUDE OF THE FOUNDER OF THE DANISH HOUSE

HARK! WE HAVE heard of the glory of the kings of men among the spear-bearing Danes† in days of long ago. We have heard how the princes won renown!

Scyld of Scefing often wrested mead†-benches from bands of enemies; he struck fear in the chieftains of many tribes. A foundling was he when he first lay friendless; fate later brought him solace as he waxed in power and flourished in wealth, until folk who lodge on the whale-paths near and far heeded his decree and gave him tribute—that was a good king!

An heir was later born to him—a son in his halls sent by heaven to comfort the people. God knew the woe they had earlier experienced when they lacked a leader, and the Lord of Life, the Wielder of Wonder, endowed the heir with renown. Beow was famed; the son of Scyld's tale spread far in the Scedelands. It is fitting that a young prince use wealth thus in his younger days while his father still lives; graciously giving so that when war comes in his later years, willing warriors come to his aid and comrades hold steadfast and loyal. Praiseworthy deeds are the ways to attain honor in every clan.

†Terms marked in the text with (†) can be looked up in the Glossary for additional information.

At the hour of destiny, stalwart Scyld departed to God's keeping. His dear clansmen carried him to the seashore, as he had bid them do while he still ruled over the Scyldings with words; he was a well-loved chieftain, and long was his tenure as lord.

In the harbor rode a ship, its prow bedecked with rings; ice-flecked, outbound—it was a prince's barge—and there they laid their beloved lord, the ring-giver, on the boat's bosom, by the mast. Many treasures and ornaments fetched from afar were gathered with him. Never have I heard of a ship so nobly adorned with weapons of war and battle gear, blades and armored mail—heaped upon him was a hoard meant to travel hence with him into the watery realm. They loaded him with gifts no less lordly than those given him when he was sent forth alone as a suckling child on the waves. And, high over his head, they set a golden banner, then gave him to the ocean, and let the waves take him; their hearts were grave, and their mood mournful. No man can truly say, neither son of the halls nor hero under heaven, who received that burden.

C H A P T E R   I

THEN THE TASK of keeping the strongholds fell to Beow, well-loved by the Scyldings. Long he ruled in fame after his father left the world, 'till in time an heir was born to him: the noble Healfdene, sage and warlike, who ruled the gracious Scyldings while he lived. Four children in succession awoke into the world from him, the chieftain of armies: Heorogar, Hrothgar, Halga the good, and Elan; I heard she was queen and dear helpmate of Ongentheow, the warlike Scylfing.

To Hrothgar was given the glories of war and such honor in combat that all his kin took him as leader, and his band of young comrades grew great. It came to his mind to order his men to build a hall, a master mead-house far mightier than any seen by the sons of earth, and therein would he bestow to young and old all that the Lord should give him, save people's land and the lives of men.

I heard that orders to craft the gathering place were widely sent to many tribes throughout the earth. His plan achieved with swiftness, that hall, the greatest of buildings, stood there ready. He, whose words held dominion in many lands, gave it the name Heorot. Nor did he go back on his promise, but distributed rings and treasure at the banquet. The hall towered high, with pinnacles spanning the sky, as it awaited the scathing blasts of deadly flame. The day had not yet come when father and son-in-law stood by with blade-baring hatred, stirred by a blood feud.

Then an evil creature who dwelt in darkness, full of envy and anger, was tormented by the hall's jubilant revel day by day, as the harps resounded loud, and the song of the singer called out clearly. The singer sang with the knowledge of tales from man's primeval time: how the Almighty fashioned the earth—a radiant plain rimmed by water—and delighted in its splendor; how He set the sun and moon as lights for the inhabitants of the land, adorned the earth's expanses with tree limbs and leaves, and made the life of all mortal beings that breathe and move.

Thus the clan's life was one of good cheer and revel until that fiend of hell began to work evils. Grendel was this grim beast called, who haunted the moors and secluded fens; this accursed one had long dwelled with monsters since the Creator had decreed his exile. On the kin of Cain did the sovereign God avenge the slaughter of Abel; Cain gained nothing from this feud and was driven far from the sight of men for that slaughter. From him awoke all those dire breeds: ogres, elves, and phantoms that warred with God a lengthy while; He paid their wage to them!

A S SOON AS night had come, Grendel set out to explore the lofty abode and to mark how the Ring-Danes had gone to rest within it after their revelry was done. He found the regal band sleeping inside after the feast, unaware of woe or human hardship. That heathen wight was right ready: fierce and reckless, he snatched thirty thanes from their slumber, then sped homeward, carrying his spoils and roaring over his prey as he sought his lair.

At dawn, the break of day, Grendel's deeds of war were made plain to men; thus, so soon after the festivities, a voice of wailing was lifted up, and in the morning was heard a great cry. The illustrious ruler, the excellent prince, sat without mirth; he wrestled with woe—the loss of his thanes, once they traced the monster's trail, brought him grief—this contest was cruel, long, and loathsome. It was a time not longer than one night before the beast committed more murders, thinking nothing of this atrocity; such was the guilt in which he was steeped. It was easy to find men who sought rest at night in remote rooms, making their beds among the hall's bowers, once the conspicuous proof of this hell-thane's malice was made manifest. Whosoever escaped the fiend kept at a distance and put up his guard.

So he reigned in terror and raged nefariously against one and all until that majestic building stood empty, and it remained long in this state. Twelve years did the Scyldings' sovereign bear this trouble, having many woes and unending travails. Thus in time the tidings became well-known among the tribes of men through ballads of lament: how unceasing was Grendel's harassment of Hrothgar and what hate he bore him, and what murder and massacre came in the many seasons of unremittant strife. He would brook no parley with any earls of the Daneland, would make no pact of peace, nor come to agreement on the blood-gold[†]—nor did any councilman expect fitting payment for the feud from his fiendish hands. Still did the evil one, the dark death-shadow, lie in wait for old and young alike, prowling about and lurking at night on the misty moors: men know not where the haunts of these hell-wizards are.

Many were the horrors that this man-hater, this solitary prowler, often wrought—severe wrongs. He ruled Heorot, that richly decorated hall, on dark nights, but never could he approach the throne sacred to God—he was the outcast of the Lord.

The sorrow of the Scyldings' friend was sore and heart-breaking. Many times did the realm gather in council, seeking out how best the stout-hearted men could try their hand against the horrific menace. Betimes at heathen shrines they made sacrifice, asking with rites that the slayer of souls would afford them relief against their people's great pain. Thus was their custom, heathen faith; 'twas of Hell they thought in their imaginings. They knew not the Almighty, the Arbiter of actions, the mighty Lord, nor did they pay mind to Heaven's Crown, the Wielder of Wonder.

Woe to he who in wretched adversity plunges his soul in the fiery bosom; he has no consolation, nor any place to turn. But it goes well with him who may draw near to his Lord after the day of death, finding friendship in the Father's arms!

C H A P T E R 3 I I I

T HUS DID THE SON of Healfdene seethe unceasingly with those
days' woe. The wisest men could not assuage his sorrow; too
burdensome and long was that anguish upon his folk, that cruel
trial, that evil of the night.

All this did a thane of Hygelac's hear in his home; great among the
Geats,[†] he heard of Grendel's doings. During the days of his life, he was
the mightiest man of valor—stalwart and noble. He ordered that a sturdy
wave-traveler be made ready, saying that he would fain visit the valiant
king far across the swan-road; this illustrious monarch was much in need
of men! No wise man gainsaid the prince's adventure, though they loved
him dearly; they commended his daring spirit and rendered good omens.
And now the brave man chose comrades, the keenest warriors that ever he
could find, from the bands of Geats. He sought the sea vessel with these
fourteen men, and, a man skilled in the water's ways, he led them by the
land's coasts.

Time had now flown; the ship was afloat, close by the cliffs. The ready
warriors embarked; the waves churned, as did the seashore's sand. On the
ship's bosom did the men carry their mail and weapons in bright array;
the sailors shoved off, with a will sending the tight-timbered craft on its
way. Over the waters did the ship move by the wind's might, like a bird
with foam plumage, until in due time on the second day, its curved prow
had run such a course that the voyagers could now see land: gleaming
sea-cliffs, towering hills, and headlands stretching to the sea; they found
their haven and their journey had ended. The Geat clansmen then climbed

ashore; they anchored the sea vessel, their armor and battle-gear clashing; they thanked God for a peaceful passage over the sea-paths.

Then from the heights, a Scylding scout, whose task it was to watch the sea-cliffs, espied them as they bore their bright shields over the gangway with war-gear in readiness; he was seized with interest to know what manner of men these were. Directly did this thane of Hrothgar ride his steed to the strand. He shook his spear mightily and spoke with formal challenge: "Who then are you, men bearing arms and clad in coats of mail, who have thus come with this mighty vessel over the ocean's ways? I have been set as a sentinel over this seacoast that no foe of the Danish folk should harm the land with marauding ships. Never have shield-bearing men so openly landed, nor do you know our clan's word of passage, or hold my folk's consent—never have I seen in the world a warrior like that one among yourselves—a hero in his armor! He is no henchman, unless his looks deceive; he has a regal bearing. Now must I know your nationality before you wander hence from here as intruders in Danish lands. Now, foreigners who fare on the ocean, hear me out: it's best to make haste and let me know from whence you come."

CHAPTER IV

THE FOREMOST MAN gave answer, and the warriors' leader unlocked his word-hoard: "We are kinsmen of the Geats' clan and are Hygelac's own hearth-fellows. My father was known to far-off folk: Ecgtheow was his name. A man of many winters, he departed as an aged man from the earth and is honored even today by sage men throughout the world's width. We come with good intent to your lord and liege, to Healfdene's son who protects his people. Be good and advise us! We come to the Danish lord with a great message, and, as I see it, nothing should remain hidden. Tell us if you know the truth about what we hear men say: that among the Scyldings a strange monster, doing black deeds in the dark of night, wreaks havoc and murder with unmatched rage and hatred. I would bring Hrothgar generous aid, that he who is wise and brave may best his foes—if ever there is to be an end to his ills and the fight that afflicts him, if a cure is to come, and the seethings of torment grow calm again—lest he suffer ever after in days of anguish and sore distress for as long as that majestic house rests high on its hill!"

Astride his steed, the shore-warden gave the answer of an undaunted clansman: "The quick-witted one must have skill to know the measure of words and deeds if he means to do well. I gather that this band is of a gracious mind toward the Scylding lord. March then with your arms and armor on the way I show you. I will order my men to guard your boat in the meanwhile, the freshly pitched ship there by the ocean's shore. They will watch it faithfully 'till it once more wends its way over the waters, bearing her well-loved lord to the Geats' borders with those that fate shall grant to pass through battle unscathed."

They then set on their march—the ship lay still, riding on her cable; the broad-bosomed boat lay fast at anchor. The boar-figures on their cheek-guards shone; forged with gold, ornate and gleaming brightly, they guarded the man of war. The heroes marched in haste 'till they saw the hall, broad-gabled and bright with gold; among earth-dwellers this majestic house was most renowned, and the light of it illuminated far-off lands. The stalwart warrior pointed to that scintillating fortress and bade them go straight there; then he wheeled his steed about like a mighty warrior, and gave a parting word: "It is time for me to go from you. May the Almighty Father guard you well with grace and mercy in your quest. I go seaward to keep my watch against hostile marauders."

C H A P T E R   5   V

THE STREET WAS stone and guided the band of men. Their coats of mail gleamed; hand-forged and hard, the steel rings on their armor sang as they marched in battle garb to the hall. The sea-weary men set down their broad shields, the stout bucklers, along the wall. Seating themselves on the bench, their breastplates and war-gear clanged. They stacked together their gray-tipped spears of ash—those men of iron had weapons worthy of them!

A proud warrior there questioned the heroes about their home and kinsmen: "Whence do you bear these burnished shields, gray armor, and grim helmets, and a multitude of spears? I am Hrothgar's herald and marshal. Never have I met so many foreigners of heroic bearing. Methinks that it's for glory—not because of exile, but for courageous valor—that you seek Hrothgar!"

To him the proud leader of the Geats made answer beneath his hardy helm: "We are of Hygelac's clan; I am named Beowulf. I seek to explain my mission to the son of Healfdene, the mighty prince and your lord, if it be his pleasure that we now greet him who is good."

Then Wulfgar, the Wendel chief well-known to many for his might of mind, courage, and wisdom, said: "I will tell the king of the Danes, the Scyldings' friend, the giver of rings, what it is that you ask; I'll tell the illustrious prince of your journey here, bringing back quickly such answer as the mighty monarch may be pleased to give."

He then made haste to where Hrothgar sat, white-haired and old with his warriors about him, 'till with gallant stance, he stood before the shoulders of the Danish king—he knew the customs of court.

Wulfgar addressed his liege: "Men from afar have come hither over the ocean's paths—people of the Geats—and the most noble of their band is named Beowulf. They seek the boon of speaking with you, my lord. Do not deny them a hearing, most gracious Hrothgar! By their war-gear they appear worthy warriors, and their leader, a hero who led his band hither, is surely a valiant man."

CHAPTER VI

HROTHGAR, THE CROWN of the Scyldings, spoke: "I knew him from his young days; his aged father was named Ecgtheow, to whom Hrethel the Geat gave his only daughter. It is surely their offspring that comes hither to visit a steadfast friend. And surely did the seamen say—those who carried my gifts thither to the Geatish court—that he has the strength of thirty men in his grip and is bold in battle. The blessèd God in His mercy has sent this man to the Western Danes as a hope against Grendel's terror. I must grant the brave youth treasures for his greatheartedness. Be quick, and bid the band of kinsmen come before me. Say to them that they are welcome guests of the Danish folk."

Wulfgar declared the word at the hall's door: "To you has my lord, the king of the Eastern Danes, sent this message: He knows your noble kin, and he bids you welcome from over the ocean's waves! Now may you go in your warlike attire, with helm on head, to greet Hrothgar; let your war-shields abide here with the wooden spears until your parley is at its end." Then the mighty one rose up with his men about him, a brave band of thanes; some remained there to guard the battle-gear, as their leader commanded. Then did that band go where the herald led them beneath Heorot's roof. Standing near the hearth, the hero spoke from beneath his helm—his coat of mail gleamed, a war-net woven by the smith's skill—"Hail, Hrothgar! My followers and I are Hygelac's kinsmen. I have gained much fame in my youth! These deeds of Grendel have been heralded clearly in my homeland. Seafaring men say that this hall, best among halls, lies empty of your thanes and useless when the evening sun is hidden away in heaven's harbor. So did the best of my people, sagacious among men, advise me to seek you here, noble Hrothgar, because they know full well the strength of my might. They themselves were witnesses when I came from battle, flecked with my foes' blood; there I bound five beasts and bested the brood of giants. I slew beasts by night on the waves, avenging at my own peril the Geats, whose woe they sought—I crushed these grim ones. Grendel, this cruel monster, will now be mine to best in single battle! And so I seek from you, sovereign of the glorious Danes, bulwark of the Scyldings, a boon—and, friend of the peoples, shield of the warriors, do not refuse it now that I've come from afar—that I alone, with my liegemen here, this stalwart band, may purge Heorot! I also hear that this fell beast in his swaggering despises weapons, and, therefore, I shall forgo the same— and in this as well, may Hygelac also be beneficent to me—and will bear neither sword nor buckler nor gold-colored shield, but with my hand's grip, I will face the fiend and fight for life, foe against foe. There shall the one taken by death resign himself to the Lord's doom."

"I suppose that, if he wins the fight, he will in this golden hall fearlessly devour my Geatish band, as he often did before to those most noble thanes. Nor then will you need to shroud my head, as I will then be his, if death takes me, gory and bloody—he'll take my bloodstained body away as prey, and that lone vagrant will ruthlessly devour it while my life's blood reddens his lair in the fen; you'll have no need to care for my corpse! If battle takes me, send to Hygelac the peerless armor that protects my breast, most stalwart of vests, heirloom of Hrethel and work of Wéland. Destiny will go as she must."

CHAPTER VII

HROTHGAR, CROWN OF the Scyldings, spoke: "To give us your pledge and rescue us at honor's call, my friend Beowulf, you have come to us. Your father's battle kindled a mighty feud when he killed Heatholaf of the Wylfings; his clansmen could not keep him for fear of invasion. Fleeing, he sought our South-Dane folk, those honorable Scyldings, over the ocean's swells, when I had first become king of the Danish folk and had dominion over the heroic treasure hoard. Heorogar, my elder brother, was dead and had breathed his last; Healfdene's son, he was better than I! Directly did I settle the feud for a price, sending ancient treasures over the wave crests to the Wylfings, and he swore fealty to me."

"It is sorrow to my soul to say to any mortal man what horrors Grendel has maliciously brought upon me in Heorot with his vicious tactics. The people of my hall, my warriors, are reduced to nothing; Destiny has swept them away in Grendel's grasp. But God is able to halt the deeds of this deadly fiend! Those warriors often boasted, when refreshed by beer from their ale mugs, that they would meet Grendel's onset with a clash of swords. Then this mead-house at the morning's tide was bespattered with gore; when daylight broke, the boards of the benches reeked of blood, and the hall was gory. I had fewer trustworthy liegemen and heroic comrades once death had robbed me of them. But sit now at the banquet and be free with your words, stalwart hero, as your heart moves you."

Then a table in the mead hall was cleared for the Geatish men, and they sat down with strong spirits and stout hearts. A servant attended them with a carved cup from which he poured the clear mead. At times the minstrel's song resonated in Heorot; heroes made merry, and there was no dearth of warriors, both Geatish and Danish.

CHAPTER VIII

UNFERTH, THE SON of Ecglaf who sat at the feet of the Scylding's lord, spoke quarrelsome words. The quest of Beowulf, that noble mariner, galled him greatly, for he always begrudged other men who might achieve more fame under heaven than he himself. "Are you that Beowulf, Breca's rival, who strove with him in swimming the open sea, pridefully braving the floods and foolishly risking your lives in the deep waters? Nor could any friend or foe dissuade you from swimming the dangerous main. You covered the ocean tides with your arms, measuring the sea-streets with strained hands, and swam over the waters while buffeted about by the ocean's roll. You strove in the sea-realm for seven nights, and he bested you in swimming and covered more of the main. Then at the morning's tide the swells cast him on the shores of the Heathoram people, whence he made for the dear home of his own beloved liegemen, the fair land of the Brondings, where he ruled his folk's towns and treasures. In triumph over you, Beanstan's son achieved his boast. I anticipate worse luck for your adventure—though you've braved the blows of battle in grim struggle—if you wait through the night of Grendel's approach!"

Beowulf, son of Ecgtheow, spoke: "What mighty things you've just said of Breca and his triumph, my dear Unferth, while you're drunk with beer! I say in truth that I have proved more might in the sea than any other man, and more endurance in the ocean. The two of us had talked in our youth and bragged—we were still mere boys then—that we would risk our lives far out at sea, and so we did it. We held drawn blades in our hands as we swam along, hoping to guard ourselves against the whale-beasts. He could not float any farther over the waters' flood than I, nor hasten more over the billows; and neither could I abandon him. The two of us stayed together on the sea for five nights until the flood parted us, and churning waves, chilly weather, the dark night, and a fierce northern wind rushed upon us, and the waves were rough. The wrath of the sea-fish was stirred, and my coat of mail, hard and hand-linked, availed me much protection against the monsters—the battle-vest was bound to my breast and decorated with gold. A fierce creature held me firm and pulled me to the bottom with the strongest grip. Nevertheless, it was granted to me that I pierce the monster with my sword point; by my hand and battle-blade was the giant sea-beast conquered.

C H A P T E R *9* I X

"AND SO OFTEN as the throngs of evil beasts assailed me, I gave them their due recompense with sword thrusts! In no way could they revel in any slaughter, nor devour me as they sat and feasted at the bottom of the sea, but at daybreak, they lay beached at the ocean's edge, sorely wounded by my blade and put to sleep with my sword. And since then they have never molested seafarers on the fathomless sea-paths.

"Light, the bright beacon of God, came from the east. The waves grew calm, and I could see the high sea-cliffs, those windy walls. Destiny often rescues the warrior not doomed to die if he has courage! And so it was that I killed nine water-monsters with my sword. I never heard of a battle more hard-fought by night beneath heaven's roof, nor of a man more desolate while adrift in the deep! Yet I escaped unharmed from the clutches of my foes, although I was weary from swimming. The sea, that swirling flood, cast me up with billowing waters on Finnish lands. I never heard of you dealing in such deadly battles, such sword-clashes. Neither Breca nor you in your playing at war have achieved such valorous deeds with flashing swords—I don't boast of those—although you were the bane of your dear brother, your closest kin, for which the curse of hell awaits you, regardless of your cunning wit! For I say in truth, son of Ecglaf, that Grendel, the fell beast, would never have wrought these grim deeds on your dear lord; Heorot would not have such havoc if your battle were as bold as your boast is loud! But he has found that he need not fear reprisal in sword-clashes with your Danish clan, your people, the mighty Scyldings. He takes blackmail and respects no one from the Danish lands, but murders for sport, fighting and feasting with not a thought of conflict with the Spear-Danes. But now I shall quickly prove to him the prowess and pride of the Geats in the ways of battle. Thereafter, he that can go to the mead-hall will merrily do so when the light of another day dawns on men as the sun, robed in radiance, shines from the south!"

The jewel-giver was then joyous; white-haired and brave in war, he awaited the help of the prince of the glorious Danes. The shepherd of the people perceived a firm resolve in Beowulf. Then the laughter of liegemen resounded loud, and jovial words were spoken.

Wealhtheow, queen of Hrothgar, came forward; mindful of ceremonies, she greeted the hall's guests in her golden garb, and handed the cup first to the sovereign of the Eastern Danes, bidding him be blithe at the banquet, as he was dear to all in the land. He, that king famed in battle, heartily took to the banquet and the cup. The Helming princess then went through the hall, carrying the cup to young and old in every part, until the moment came when the ring-adorned queen with noble heart bore the mead-cup to Beowulf. She greeted the leader of the Geats, thanking God with wise words that her will was granted and that at long last her hope could rest upon a hero for comfort amid terrors. The mighty warrior took the cup from Wealhtheow's hand and spoke about his eagerness for combat. Beowulf, son of Ecgtheow, said: "My intention upon coming on board our boat and taking to the ocean with my comrades was to fully accomplish the will of your people—or to fall in battle to my death in the grip of the fiend. I resolved to do heroic deeds or to end the days of my life right here in the mead-hall." These words, Beowulf's battle-boast, pleased the woman. Bright with gold, the noble lady sat by her lord.

Then the hall held mighty words and the sounds of a throng as it had at first, and the proud band made merry until the son of Healfdene was of a mind to seek rest for the night. He knew that a fight with the fiend in that festal hall awaited the hour when the sun shone no more and the dark shroud of night came over all, when shadowy shapes stalk abroad, warring in obscurity. To a man, the warriors rose up; he spoke man-to-man, did Hrothgar to Beowulf, and wished him luck while granting him command in the mead-hall, adding these words: "Since I could lift up hand and shield, I never before trusted the guardianship of this noble Dane-Hall to any man—except to you on this occasion. Have now and hold this peerless house; remember your fame and be valiant; keep watch for the foe! No desire of yours will be unfulfilled if you come through the battle boldly with your life."

C H A P T E R   X

T HEN HROTHGAR, SHIELD of the Scyldings, went forth from the hall with his retinue of men; the warlord desired to lie with Wealhtheow his queen. The glorious king had set a guard against Grendel—so the men told one another—a defender of the hall who protected the monarch and watched for the monster. In truth, the prince of the Geats gladly trusted in his valorous might and the mercy of God!

He then cast off his iron corselet and the helmet on his head, and gave to his esquire the richly-gilt sword, the best of weapons, giving him command to guard the battle-gear. He then spoke vaunted words to the valiant men before he sought the bed: "I reckon myself to be in the ready for grim deeds of war, and in no way weaker than Grendel. For this reason will I not give his life to the sleep of death with a sword, although I could. He has no skill to strike me with sword or hew through shield, mighty though he may be in his horrific feats. We shall both spurn the sword this night if he dares to seek me here and make war without weapons. Let the wise God, the holy Lord, decree success on whichever side seems right to Him!"

Then the warrior reclined, and the pillow received the face of the prince, while all about him many stout sea-warriors sank into their beds in the hall. None thought their steps would ever go thence back to the people and the fortresses that fostered them, to the lands they loved. They knew full well that death in battle had seized many warriors of the Danish clan in the banquet hall. But the Lord granted them comfort and help, weaving a good web of war for the Geatish folk that, by the might of one, the strength of a single man, they might prevail against their enemy. It is said truly by all that God has ever governed over mankind!

He came striding in the dim night, the shadow-walker. The defenders, whose charge it was to guard the gabled hall, all slept—save one.

It was widely known that the marauder could not hurl him into darkness against God's will, yet even so he, vigilant against the foe, awaited, bold and full of warrior's wrath, for the battle's outcome.

C H A P T E R X I

THEN GRENDEL CAME from the moors by way of the misty crags; God's wrath lay heavy on him. The monster was of a mind to seize a human in the noble hall. He walked beneath the clouds towards the mead-hall until he saw with glee the golden hall of men with its gilded woodwork. This was not the first time that he'd sought Hrothgar's homestead, but never before had he found such mighty warriors, such guardians of the hall!

The accursèd rogue then came to the hall; the door opened when his fists struck it, even though it had been fastened with bolts of iron, and he ripped open the house's mouth in his furious rage. He then quickly tread over the paved floor, his ire streaming like flashes from his eyes, like a flame. He spied the band of heroes in the hall, the hardy liegemen, that group of clansmen gathered together sleeping. Then his heart laughed, for the savage beast was in the mood to sever each soul's life from its body before daybreak as he saw this opportunity to sate his slaughterous appetite. But Destiny did not permit him to seize any more of mankind after that evening.

The mighty kinsman of Hygelac closely watched his cursèd foe to see how the assassin would advance. Nor was the monster inclined to hesitate, but he promptly seized a sleeping warrior in his first move, tore him fiercely asunder, bit his frame of bones, drank the blood of his veins, and swallowed large morsels; momentarily, the lifeless corpse was devoured—feet, hands, and all. Then he stepped further in, grasping at Beowulf with his hand, feeling with a fiendish claw for the reclining hero—who boldly grasped him, returning in kind with a grip on the arm. Then the master of evil saw that he was in a man's grip, stronger than any he had ever met on the whole earth; his heart quailed, and he became alarmed—he could not escape soon enough! He wanted to flee and seek his lair, that devil's den. He could not now do what he had often done in days of long ago! Then the brave thane of Hygelac thought upon his evening's boast, and he bounded up and grasped firm his foe, whose fingers cracked in breaking. The fiend was making off, but the prince followed close behind. The monster desired to fling himself free, if at all he could, and fly far away to the fens—he knew that his fingers' power was in the grip of a fearsome foe; this was a dire march to Heorot that this devastating beast had made!

A din filled the hall, and the ale-sleep left all the Danes, castle-dwellers, clansmen, and princes. Both the champions were enraged, and the building resounded with the strain of their struggle; it was a wonder that the mead-hall stood firm, and that the fair house fell not to the ground—for it was fastened within and without with iron bands of cunning smithy-skill. Even so, many gold-decorated mead-benches crashed from the sill where the grim foes wrestled. The wisest Scylings had believed that no man's might would ever break apart that stout, bone-carved house or unhinge it by any means—unless a fire's embrace should engulf it in smoke.

The clamor redoubled its intensity, and each and every Dane of the North was stricken with terrible fear, even those out on the wall, when they heard the wailing when God's foe let fly his dismal song, the cry of defeat, as hell's servant howled in pain. He who among men was greatest in might during his life's days held him too tightly.

CHAPTER XII

H E WHO WAS the earl's defender would in no way allow the murderous stranger to live, and he did not consider his days or years useful to any man on earth. Now many of Beowulf's band brandished ancestral blades, wanting to save the life of their leader, the proud prince, if such they could do. They did not know as they neared their foe, those stalwart warriors who thought to hack him on every side and kill the accurséd one, that not even the keenest blade or the best falchion fashioned on earth could hurt or harm that hideous fiend! His sorceries made him safe from the victorious sword and all iron edges. His departure from life and his end would be full of woe, and his departed spirit would wander far off into the fiends' domain. He, who in former days had wrought such murder on many men, whose heart was full of harm and hatred of God, soon found that his mortal body now failed him. The valiant kinsman of Hygelac now held him by the hand; each one's life was loathsome to the other. The foul bandit took a mortal wound, and a fatal tear appeared on his shoulder. His sinews ripped apart and his bone-frame broke. Victory was now given to Beowulf, and Grendel, sick unto his death, went hence and sought his den in the dark moors, that vile abode; he knew full well that his life had reached its end and that the last of his days on earth had come. The fulfillment of the desire of all Danes had come through the bloody battle.

He who came from afar, stalwart and wise, had purged Hrothgar's hall of ravage; his night work–brilliant and honorable–had succeeded. The valiant Geat had made good his boast to the Eastern Danes, assuaging all their sorrow and ills, and the harrowing struggle which they had endured for so long, forced to suffer that great indignity. Proof of this—the hand, arm, and shoulder of Grendel, his full, strong grip —was displayed beneath the high gabled roof.

CHAPTER XIII

THEN, AS MEN tell me the story, many warriors gathered in the
morning around the gift-hall, leaders from far and near came by
the wide roads to view the wonder, those traces of the hated one.
The end of his life was no grief to any man who surveyed the tracks of the
downed foe, how he, weary-hearted and bested in battle, doomed to death
and a fugitive, fled in fear to the devil's mere. The surface there surged with
blood, and the turbid tide of tumbling waves seethed with reeking gore
spilled by the sword—he, doomed to death, had dyed it, and, forlorn, had
yielded up his life in a boggy den; hell received his heathen soul there.

Then gray-haired clansmen, many youths, and stalwart warriors rode
back in high spirits on horses from the mere, and Beowulf's victory was
recounted. Many a man said that among all the seas of the world, south or
north, that none of the other shield-bearing warriors under the expanse of
heaven's vault were more valiant or more worthy to rule! They did not at
all, however, disparage their gracious lord Hrothgar—he was a good king!

Now and then, the experienced warriors set their gray steeds to gallop,
running a race when the roadways seemed fair or were well-known.
Otherwise, a thane of the king who had told many tales and whose mind
was full of sagas and songs of the old world began anon to bind words
together in a well-knit rhyme, forging his tale; and this thane soon sang
quite cleverly of Beowulf's quest. He detailed at length the war-like deeds
heard in Sigemund's saga. Therein were many strange things, and he said
them all: the Waelsing's wide wanderings, his battles which were never told
to the tribes of men, the feuds and atrocities he faced with none but Fitela

by his side, and how he never spoke as uncle to nephew of these things as they stood by one another in every conflict. They laid low many of the monster's spawn with their swords.

After Sigemund's death-day, no little fame arose for him, mighty in battle, who had vanquished a dragon that kept the treasure; he, the prince, was under the ancient rock when he ventured this perilous deed alone—Fitela was not with him. Nevertheless, it so happened that his sword pierced through that wondrous worm 'till the mighty blade struck the wall, and the dragon died in its blood. Thus had the fearsome warrior achieved by daring the mastery of the jewel-hoard, and the son of Waels loaded the boat, putting the shining gold on the ship's bosom; the worm was consumed by heat. Of all heroes, he had the highest renown among the races of men, and was the shelter-of-warriors because of the daring deeds that adorned his name after the hand and heart of King Heremod grew weak in battle. He was promptly banished and lured into ambush by his powerful foes; he was betrayed to death. Floods of sorrow had weakened him for too long, and he proved a worry to all his liegemen. Moreover, in his earlier days, many wise clansmen mourned the wayfaring life of this warrior, hoping to have help from grief and harm through him, thinking that the sovereign's son would wax powerful and take his father's place in protecting his people, the treasure, the stronghold, and the heroes' land, the Scyldings' home. Hygelac's kinsman here seemed more acceptable to all the people—this other, Heremond, was seized with villainy!

At times, they raced with their swift steeds on the fallow roads. The morning sun climbed higher. Many clansmen hastened to the high-vaulted hall, eager to witness the wonder. The king himself, guardian of the treasure, came with regal bearing from his bower with his retainers; his queen and her crowd of ladies walked the path to the fair mead-hall.

C H A P T E R   X I V

HROTHGAR SPOKE WHEN he went to the hall and stood on the steps. He looked at the steep roof decorated with gold and saw Grendel's hand: "For this sight we must make thanksgiving to the Sovereign Ruler without delay! I have endured a host of sorrows from Grendel, but God, the Lord of Glory, works wonder upon wonder! Earlier, I thought I would never see help for my woes as long as I lived, with this noble house standing soaked in blood and stained with sword-gore. The travail had scattered all my counselors, who had no hope of ever rescuing this people's hall from the spiteful demons and beasts.

"Now has this hero, through God's might, done a deed which we for all this time were unable to do with our wisdom and cunning. Lo! Well can she among women who bore this warrior among all the sons of man say, if she still lives, that the God of ages was good to her in the birth of her son.

"Now, Beowulf, best of heroes, I shall heartily love you as if you were mine own son. Preserve this new friendship from this time forth. Nothing in the world that you desire will you lack, so long as it is within my power. Often have I promised recompense for lesser deeds and given my precious hoard to a hero less famed who was less ready to fight.

"By your deeds, you have ensured that your fame shall endure through all the ages. May the Almighty ever reward you with good, just as He has now done!"

Beowulf, son of Ecgtheow, spoke: "We have fought this work of war most willingly and fearlessly dared the unknown. I would that you had seen it yourself, the fiend in all his gear, tottering to fall! I thought to bind him down on his deathbed swiftly with my strong grip, that he should breathe his last in my grasp, but he broke away and I could not, as the Maker did not will it, halt his flight. The life-destroyer was too overpowering in his escape. However, he left his hand, arm, and shoulder in payment for his rescue. He has not, however, bought reprieve with this, nor will he live the longer for it, the loathsome fiend steeped in sins. The wound has him bound closely in the grip of agony, in baleful bonds, where the crime-stained wretch must await such awful doom as the Ancient One may allot him."

The son of Ecglaf was more silent in the boasting of his battle-deeds, as all the thanes beheld that hand because of the great prowess of the prince. Gazing at the high roof, the foe's fingers were spread, and each nail was likened unto steel; the heathen warrior's claw was uncanny, having horrific spikes as a hand-spear. It was clear, they said, that no blade of ancient design, however keen, could sever that bloody hand of battle from the evil foe.

C H A P T E R   X V

THEN THE ORDER was given to promptly bedeck the hall of
Heorot, and the throng of men and women who gathered to gar-
nish the mead hall and bowers was dense. The tapestries glistened
like gold, with many scenes of wonder that delighted each mortal who
looked upon them. Though strengthened with iron bonds, the bright
building was badly broken. The door-hinges were torn, and the roof alone
remained intact when, ridden with guilt, the fiend fled for his life.

It is no small task to escape death, for those who try it! For all soul-
bearing folk among the races of men and earth-dwellers are forced to that
fated place where, after the feast, their body sleeps on its deathbed.

Then the hour arrived when Healfdene's son proceeded to the hall:
the king himself would share the feast. Never have I heard that a greater
host of that nation gathered graciously 'round their ring-giver! Those
who owned renown sat at the benches to enjoy the feast, and the mighty
in spirit quaffed many a cup of mead with the kinsmen in the sumptuous hall, Hrothgar and Hrothulf. Heorot was now filled with friends; no
Scylding folk had yet attempted treachery.

Then did the son of Healfdene present to Beowulf a banner woven of
gold as an ensign for the victory, an embroidered flag of battle, a helmet
and a coat of mail, and a precious sword that was seen by many when they
brought it before the hero. Beowulf drank the cup of thanks in the hall, for
he had no need to be ashamed of those gifts of bounty before the throngs
of warriors. I have heard of few heroes in such a hearty mood being thus
honored with four such gold-decorated gifts at the ale-bench! About the

top of the helmet, there was fixed a ridge of wire to ward the head, lest sharp battle-blades scathe it when that shield-bearing hero should grapple with fierce foes.

The shielder of the people commanded that eight steeds with carved headgear be led into the court; one horse had a gleaming saddle set with jewels; it was the battle-seat of the high king, when the son of Healfdene was of a mind to exercise with swords. His valor never failed when the corpses fell in the battlefront. And so, the chief of Ing's descendants gave both to Beowulf at once, the steeds and the weapons, and wished him well in enjoying them. And so manfully did the great king, keeper of the hoard and heroes, recompense that hard battle with horses and treasures, that none who knew truth could ever condemn him.

CHAPTER XVI

AND THE LORD of warriors gave to each of Beowulf's fellow voyagers a precious gift, an heirloom, and ordered that the blood-price be paid in gold for the one whom Grendel had killed—and he would have killed more of them, had not the Providence of God and Fate—along with the valor of man—barred his way. The Ancient One ruled mankind then as he does now and always. Therefore, it is always best to have prudence and insight of mind. He who long sojourns through war-filled days in this world will have much of both pleasure and pain.

Then did the song and music mingle together in the presence of Healfdene's war-prince, and harpsong of the hero's ballad was heard as Hrothgar's bard invoked joy in the mead-hall and on the ale-benches by playing the song of that sudden raid on the Finnish sons: "Hnaef the Scylding, Healfdene's hero, was doomed to fall in the Frisian† slaughter."

"Hildeburh had no cause to value her enemies' honor! She lost both loved ones at the shield-clashing; both son and brother were innocent. Fate took them; they were stricken by spears, and she was mournful. None doubted why Hôc's daughter bewailed her fate when dawn came and she saw them lying under the sky, her kinsmen murdered, where she had 'till now enjoyed the world's blessings.

"Finn's own liegemen were also cut down by war, and few were left on the battlefield; he could no longer raise weapon or wage war on Hengest and rescue his band's remnants by might from the king's thane. He offered Hengest a pact: The Danes would have another hall and throne, and half the power should go to those in Frisian lands. When time came for tribute,

43

Finn, Folcwald's son, would favor Hengest's folk by day with rings, even honoring them with as much treasure, jewels, and beaten gold as he in his own mead-hall honored his Frisian folk. Thereupon they plighted a treaty of peace on both sides. Finn swore to Hengest upon his honor to rule the woeful remnant by wise law, governing them nobly so that no man among them would break the treaty—they now followed the slayer of their ring-giver with minds full of malice and mourning, forced to do this, as was their fate. Should any Frisian with the taunt of a foe recall this murderous hatred to mind, the sword-edge would seal his doom. The oath was sworn, and heaps of ancient gold were brought from the hoard.

"The stalwart Scylding, best among the warriors, lay upon his funeral pyre. On the fires were clearly seen the bloody hauberks, the gilded swine-crests, the iron boars and the many princes slain by the sword; many had fallen in battle. Hildeburh gave orders that her own son's body should be committed to the flames at Hnaef's pyre, his bones burning at his uncle's side. The woman wept in woeful lamentations, and the war-hero soared in flames. The largest of death-fires climbed to the clouds, roaring over the hillock: heads melted, gashes burst, and blood gushed out of the body's wounds. The doomfire, that greedy demon, devoured them all, those spared not by war; the springtime bloom of both folk was gone."

C H A P T E R   X V I I

"THEN WARRIORS HASTENED to their homes; bereft of friends, they returned to the Frisian land, the homesteads and high fortresses. Hengest yet remained with Finn during that bloodstained winter, honoring the pact and thinking of his home. He was powerless to drive the ring-covered prow of his ship over the waters, as now the waves rolled fiercely with lashing winds or stood locked in winter's icy chains. Then another year came upon the dwellings of man, as even now it continues to do—skies bright with sun always come in their season. Winter was driven far off, and the earth's bosom was fair. That adventurer was up and ready to depart, leaving where he had been guest.

"However, he thought more upon revenge than on sea-roving, and how to hasten hot encounters with the sons of the Frisians. And so he, too, was doomed when Hunlafing gave the scintillating blade of battle to him, the best of blades; its edges were feared among enemies. And in this manner, the sword-death fell upon the fierce-hearted Finn while he was at home; after their sea-voyage, Guthlaf and Oslaf recounted many tales of woe, and so Finn's wild spirit stayed not within his breast. The fortress was red with the blood of enemies, and Finn was slain, the king amid his guards; the queen was taken. The Scylding warriors carried to their ship all the king's possessions and anything of gems and jewels they found in Finn's domain. The gentle wife was carried back over the sea-paths to the Danes."

The lay, that bardic ballad, was sung to its end. Then the glad feast rose, and the sound of merriment grew bright. Cup-bearers poured wine from their wondrous flagons. Wealtheow then came forward, moving beneath her golden diadem to where the two brave men sat, uncle and nephew, each true to the other in kindred affection. Unferth the orator sat at the feet of the Scylding lord; men had faith in Unferth's spirit and the might of his courage, although in swordfighting he had been disloyal to his kin.

The Scyldings' lady spoke: "Drink of this cup, my lord, giver of rings! Be you merry, oh magnanimous friend of men, and speak gentle words to the Geats, as men should do! Be glad with them and mindful of those gifts you've received from near and far. Men say that you wish to receive this hero as your son. Heorot has been purged; enjoy that bright hall of riches while you can, and give many treasures, leaving folk and land to your children when you must away to your fate. For I deem that my gracious Hrothulf will rule honorably over the young ones if you quit the world earlier than he does, Scyldings' friend. I believe he will repay good to our children if he remembers well all the comfort and gifts of honor that we bestowed on him when he was helpless." She then turned to the seat where her sons were placed, Hrethric and Hrothmund, the two young sons of heroes; the Geat also sat there, brave Beowulf, between the brothers.

C H A P T E R   X V I I I

S HE GAVE A CUP to him, and spoke kindly words of greeting to him. Wrought gold was also graciously presented to him: two armlets, a ringéd corselet, and a collar the likes of which I've never heard of in the world. Never beneath heaven's hall have I heard of so mighty a hero's gem-hoard, not since Hama bore away the Brisings' necklace to the bright fortress—with jewels and casket, he fled Eormenric's hatred and chose eternal reward.

Hygelac the Geat, grandson of Swerting, carried that collar on his last raid, defending his prize and guarding the war-spoil beneath his banner until Fate overwhelmed him, for he in his daring did seek danger and feuded with the Frisians. He carried the fair gem over the ocean's cup, did that mighty chieftain, and he died beneath his shield. His corpse, the cuirass, and the gorgeous collar all came under the power of the Frankish King; the weaker warriors won the spoil from the Geatland's lord and people, who held the field of death. A din rose in the hall.

Amid the warriors, Wealhtheow spoke, saying: "Take joy in this collar, beloved Beowulf, and wear this cuirass! They are royal treasures. Prosper well, be mighty in valor, and be a kind advisor to these lads! I will reward you for it. You have done such deeds that men will celebrate your fame far and wide for all days, even so wide as the ocean surges and to the walls of the wind. Be happy through the ways of life, O prince! I wish you precious possessions. Be helpful in deeds to my son, and sustain his joy! Here is each warrior true to the other, kindhearted, and loyal to their king.

Thanes are cordial, the people are obedient; be merry, liegemen—listen and obey!"

She then went to her place. That was the proudest of feasts, and wine flowed for the warriors. They knew not Fate, nor the cruel destiny to be seen by many clansmen when evening came and Hrothgar took himself to his bower, the prince to his rest. The room was guarded by an army of warriors as they had often done before. They cleared the bench-boards, and the room throughout was spread with beds and bolsters. One of the revelers whose end was near lay down to rest—a doomed man in the hall. They set their war-shields, bright bucklers, at their heads; over each prince on each bench was, plain in view, the towering battle-helmet, the powerful spear, and the coat of ringéd mail. It was their way to be ever prepared for battle, whether at home or in the field—in whatever occasion their liege lord needed their services. They were good clansmen.

C H A P T E R   X I X

THEY THEN SANK into slumber. One there was who paid dearly for the evening's rest—as had often happened when Grendel occupied that golden hall, wreaking evil until his end drew nigh; he was slaughtered for sins. It became known and widely told that an avenger still lived after the fiend. Remembering this dire fight for a great while, Grendel's mother, that wife of trolls, lamented her loss. She was doomed to dwell in dreary waters and cold streams ever since Cain cut down his only brother, his father's son, with his sword-edge. He had been marked with murder and fled as an outlaw; shunned from among men, he inhabited the wilderness. From him there awoke such hellish spirits as Grendel, who, terrible wolf of war, had found at Heorot a vigilant warrior ready for battle. The fell beast grappled with him there, but the warrior remembered his mighty power, that glorious gift that God had granted him, and trusted his Maker's mercy for courage and support. In this way he conquered the enemy and felled the fiend; that foe of man fled forlorn and heartless to the realms of death. And yet now his mother, bloodthirsty and grim, would embark upon a dolorous quest to avenge her son's death.

The hag came to Heorot, where the helmeted Danes slept in the hall. The princes' old woes came back suddenly when Grendel's mother burst into their midst. Her terror, however, was less, even as a woman in war is less fearsome, and a maiden's might is lesser than that of a man-at-arms, whose hard and hammer-forged sword, stained with blood, carves through the boar on a helm's crest with its keen edge. Those hard edges were drawn in the hall, taken from where they lay on the benches, and many shields were firmly raised. Many thought neither about helmets nor mail-coats when they were surprised with terror.

That hag was in haste, wanting to flee with her life when the liegemen spotted her. However, she seized a single clansman firmly as she fled to the moors. He was the dearest of heroes to Hrothgar; a trusty vassal among the oceans was he whom she killed upon his couch—a mighty shield-warrior. Beowulf was not there—another house had been set apart for the renowned Geat after the gift-giving. Heorot was in an uproar, and the hag took the famous blood-spattered hand. Fear had come again, and there was mourning in the fortress. It was a barter of sorrow where the Danes and Geats were fated to pay with their loved ones' lives.

That venerable king, the white-haired hero, was bitter in spirit when he knew that his noble chieftain no longer lived, that the thane most dear to him was dead. Beowulf, the dauntless victor, was brought in haste to the king's bower. At daybreak, the princely lord went with his clansmen, the warriors, to where the king in his abode waited to see if the Almighty would ever turn about this woe-filled tale. He who was renowned in battle marched across the floor with his companions in arms—the hall-timbers echoed—and went to greet the wise old king, the lord of the Ingwines, to ask about whether he had passed the night in peace.

C H A P T E R　　X X

HROTHGAR, CROWN OF the Scyldings, spoke: "Ask not of pleasure! Grief is renewed for the Danish folk. Æschere, elder brother of Yrmenlaf, is dead; he was my scribe and counselor, my comrade in the heat of battle when warriors clashed, and we defended our heads as the boar-helms were hewn; each prince should be as a famed hero as Æschere was! But here in Heorot he has met his death at the hand of a ravaging spirit. I know not which return path she took, exulting in her prey on her gruesome trail. She renewed her feud, as yesternight you smothered Grendel in a grip most severe because he ruined and ravaged my liegemen for too long. His life seized, he fell in battle; now another one, cunning and cruel, has come to avenge her kin and further aggravate this blood feud. So it appears to many thanes, sorrowful in heart for their ring-giver. The hand that once fulfilled their desires is now stilled in death.

"I have heard from landowners and liegemen of mine who dwell nearby that a pair such as these has betimes been seen stalking the marches; those mighty wandering spirits haunt the moors. So far as my folk could determine, one seemed a female hag, and the other miscreant walked wretched paths of exile in a man's form, though larger than a human. The landfolk named him Grendel in days of long ago; they know not of his father, nor of the lineage of these treacherous goblins. Their home is not trodden by man; they inhabit wolf-crags, windy headlands, and dread fens where the mountain streams fall amid rocks to the gloom of an underground flood. It is not far from here as miles are measured, and there the mere stands with a frost-bound forest of sturdy roots overshadowing the water. By night, a strange wonder can be seen: fire upon those waters; no one living among the sons of men is wise enough to know the mere's depth! The stag who roves the heaths, the hart with strong horns that runs through the woods, may be driven far and pursued by hounds, but he would sooner give up life and breath on the water's edge than dare to plunge his head in. That is no happy place! From thence surge up the waves, misty unto the clouds, and the wind stirs foul weather, the air becomes thick, and the skies weep. Now our help once more rests with you alone! You do not yet know that place of fear where you'll find that guilt-ridden being. Seek it if you dare! I will reward you for waging this fight as I did before, with ancient treasure and braided gold, should you return."

C H A P T E R XXI

BEOWULF, SON OF Ecgtheow, spoke: "Do not lament, wise sire! It seems better that each man avenge his friends than to mourn them to no end. Each of us must await the end of his path in this world, and he who can, should achieve renown before death! That is the best memorial when life is past and a warrior's days are recounted. Rise up, oh warden of the realm! We ride forth promptly to catch the trail of Grendel's mother. Mark my words—she shall find no shelter, neither in the earth of the fields, nor the mountainous woods, nor the ocean's depths—wherever she may flee! Have patience and endure your woes this day, as I suspect you shall."

The gray-bearded king then rose quickly. He thanked God, the mighty Lord, for the man's brave words. A horse with curly mane was soon saddled for Hrothgar. The monarch rode forth nobly; the shielded footmen followed. Tracks were clearly seen in the woodlands and over all the ground where she had passed on the dismal moors, carrying off the dead man-at-arms who was bravest and best, who helped to rule in Hrothgar's homestead. Then did he born of princes go over steep cliffs and narrow gullies, straight and lonely paths and unknown ways, bare headlands and the haunts of water-monsters. He went foremost with a few of his wiser men to explore the ground until he found in an instant those gloomy trees hanging over the icy rock—it was a dire wood, and the turbulent waters beneath were dyed with blood. The Danish men were shocked, and many heroes among the Scyldings were tormented when they encountered

Æschere's head near the lake-cliff. The waters bubbled, and the warriors saw that it was hot with gore.

The horn sounded betimes with a bold battle-song. The company all sat down and watched many serpentine monsters and sea-drakes swimming in the deep. Water monsters such as those that wreak havoc on the sailing paths at morning were lying on the lake's edges, along with dragons and beasts. At that brazen horn's sound, they made away into the swells, enraged. The Geats' guardian separated one from life and from all swimming with an arrow from his bow; the sharp shaft of war stood fixed in its heart. The one whom death had seized swam no more; the wondrous wave-tosser was promptly dragged to the shore from the waters with boar-spears bristling with hooks and barbs. The warriors viewed this grisly beast.

Then Beowulf girded himself in the armor of battle; he was in no way fearful for his life. Now must the broad, brightly colored, and hand-crafted cuirass test the waters. It could well protect the warrior's body; the battle would break upon his breast in vain, and his heart would not be harmed by the foe's hand. Moreover, the white helmet that guarded his head was destined to dare the pool's depths and face the raging waves. It was encircled with royal wreaths and silver decorations, such as the smiths of old would wondrously craft; it was set about with boar figures so that no manner of swords brandished in battle could harm that helm.

Nor was that the least among the mighty aids which Hrothgar's orator offered: there was also a hilted sword named "Hrunting," easily the foremost among the ancient heirlooms. Its edge was iron, and it shone with serpentine etchings; it was hardened with battle-blood and had never proved false to any hero who brandished it in hand—he who held it was prepared to walk the paths of peril into the den of foes. This was not the first time it had been used to accomplish heroic tasks. For Ecglaf's son, stalwart and strong, did not bear in mind the speech he had made of late when drunk with wine—he now loaned this weapon to a stouter swordsman. He himself did not dare to risk his life as a loyal liegeman beneath the waters' tumult, and so he fell short of glory and the honor of court. It was not so with the one who now girded himself for the grim encounter.

B EOWULF, SON OF Ecgtheow, spoke: "Keep in mind, honorable son of Healfdene, gold-friend to men, and wise sovereign, what you once said: that if I should lose my life for your cause, you would be loyal to me for the sake of my father, though I fall! Be then the guardian of my group of thanes, my warrior friends, if I am taken by War; beloved Hrothgar, send to Hygelac the gifts you have given me! So will Geatland's king understand, and Hrethel's son will see, when he gazes upon the treasure, that I had won a friend famed for generosity, and took joy while I could in my bestower of jewels. And allow Unferth, thane of far-flung fame, to wield the ancient heirloom, the wondrous hard-edged sword; with Hrunting I now seek glory for myself, or death shall take me."

After these words, the lord of the Weder-Geats hastened off, not waiting for any answer. The eddying floods engulfed the hero. It took most of the day before he could reach the land at the bottom.

That grim and greedy goblin who had held the watery domain for a hundred winters soon found that one from among mankind had come from above and was exploring her realm of monsters. She reached out for him with grisly talons and seized the warrior, but she did not wound his healthy body—the breastplate prevented this, and she tried to shatter that war-cuirass of well-knit links with her loathsome fingers. Then this wolf of the waves, upon reaching the bottom, bore the ring-covered prince to her lair. Though his valor held, he struggled in vain to wield weapons against the terrifying monsters that set upon him while he swam. Many sea-beasts tried to tear his mail with fierce tusks when they swarmed upon this stranger.

He soon noticed that he was now in some strange cavern where no water could harm him and the fangs of the depths could never reach him through the roof. He saw firelight flung in beams from a bright blaze. The warrior saw that wolf of the deep, the monstrous lake-hag. He swung his blade with a mighty stroke, and did not hold back. Then the fair blade sang its wild warsong upon her head. But the warrior found that Hrunting would not bite and take life: its edge failed its noble master in time of need, even though it had known strife in many hands of old, had split helmets and war-gear of the doomed. This was the first time that the glory of the gleaming blade fell. Hygelac's kinsman stood firm and his courage did not quail, as he had exploits in mind. The wrathful warrior flung away that decorated, jewel-studded blade; steel-edged and stark, it lay upon the earth. He trusted in his strength and the grip of his mighty hand.

So should a man do whenever he thinks of earning lasting fame in battle—he will not fear for his life!

Then the lord of the war-like Geats who did not shrink from combat seized Grendel's mother by the shoulder; that fierce one filled with rage then flung his deadly foe, and she fell to the ground. She swiftly paid him back with her grisly grasp, and grappled with him. Spent with struggle, the warrior stumbled—that fiercest of fighters fell. She hurled herself on the hall's visitor, and drew her broad, brown-edged knife to avenge her only son. The braided mail about his breast prevented death, and barred point and blade from entering.

The life of the son of Ecgtheow, prince of the Geats, would have ended there underneath the wide earth if his armor of war, hard net of battle, had not aided him; and the Holy God, wisest Maker, wielded the victory. The heavenly Ruler championed his cause, and he soon stood on his feet again.

CHAPTER 23 XXIII

THEN AMONG THE battle gear there he saw a blade triumphant—
an old sword of the giants, an heirloom of warriors, a peerless
weapon. It was larger than other men could carry into battle-ban-
dying, as it had been wrought by giants. Then did he, champion of the
Scyldings, grasp the hilt of the blade and brandish the sword; heedless
of his life, he smote so ferociously that it caught her by the neck, breaking her bones. The sword pierced through the flesh of that doomed one;
she fell to the floor. The sword was gory, and the man was pleased with
his work.

Then light shone forth; it was bright in there, as when heaven's candle
shines in a sky without clouds. Then he scanned the hall, going by the wall
with his weapon raised by the hilt, fierce and aggressive. The edge was not
useless to the warrior now; he wished to promptly repay Grendel for the
many grim raids he had made in his war on the Western-Danes; far more
than just once had he done this, when he murdered Hrothgar's hearth-
companions in their slumber, devouring fifteen Danes and carrying off
an equal number—a horrible prey! The furious prince had paid him back
well for that. For he now saw Grendel lying there, weary of war and bereft
of life, for so had Heorot's battle ravaged him. The carcass opened wide,
even in death, when it received this blow: with a savage sword-strike, he
severed the head.

Soon, the observant men who, with Hrothgar, were watching the
waters saw them grow turbid; the waves were tinged with blood. Old men
with gray hair spoke together about the brave hero; they did not expect

the warrior, proud in conquest, to come seek their mighty master again. It seemed to many that the wave-wolf had taken his life.

The ninth hour of the day came. The noble Scyldings left the headland, and the gold-friend of men headed homeward. But the foreigners stayed and stared at the waves; sick at heart, they wished and yet did not expect to see their winsome lord again.

Then that sword, bloodied with battle-gore from the fight, began to waste away; it was a marvelous thing that the war-blade melted away just as ice dissolves when the Father loosens the frosty fetters, and unwinds the wave's chains—he is the true God!

That lord of the Geats did not take from those halls any precious things, though he saw much, but only the head and the jewel-encrusted hilt; the blade had already melted away, and the decorated sword had burned away, so fiercely hot was that blood, and so poisonous was the hell-spirit that perished there.

Soon he who safely saw the downfall of demons in combat was swimming and diving up through the waters. The turbulent waves in the watery domain where that wandering one had spent her life in this ephemeral world were now cleansed.

Then he who was sturdy in spirit swam to the strand; that crown among men was proud of the lake's booty, the burden that he bore bravely with him. The valiant band of thanes went to greet him, and they thanked God that they could see their chieftain safe and sound again. They soon loosed helmet and armor from that ardent hero. The mere subsided; the water under heaven was stained with war's blood.

They went forth from there by the paths they had taken earlier, passing over the highways and country roads. Those stalwart men carried the head away from the lake's cliffs—it was a daunting task for the whole company, for four strong men were required to strenuously bear Grendel's head on the spear to the golden hall. The brave adventurers presently arrived at the hall; fourteen Geats came marching, with their mighty chieftain amid them as they trod the meadow-ways. Then that prince of thanes proceeded to enter; the fearless fighting man of wide renown, the valiant hero, went to greet Hrothgar. After him, Grendel's head was borne into the hall where the men were drinking; it struck awe in the clansmen and queen alike, and the men looked upon this monstrous visage.

CHAPTER 24 XXIV

BEOWULF, SON OF Ecgtheow, then spoke: "Lo and behold! To you, son of Healfdene, lord of the Scyldings, have we heartily brought this booty from the lake; what you look upon here is a sign of victory! It was no light matter for me to escape with my life. I pursued this task with endless effort in war beneath the water, and even so my strength would have been lost had not the Lord shielded me. Aught could I accomplish with Hrunting in this work of war, even though it is a good weapon. And yet, the Lord of men granted to me that I should spy upon the wall, hanging in splendor, a gargantuan and ancient blade—how often does He guide men when they are friendless!—and with this blade did I fight, felling the hall's wardens because fate was with me. The sword of war, that bright blade, then completely melted when the blood gushed over it, the hot sweat of battle—but I brought the hilt back from my foes. Thus I avenged their fiendish deeds and the death-agony of Danes, as was fitting. And so I proclaim that you can now sleep safely in Heorot with your band of warriors, and every thane among your folk, young and old, has no evil to fear from that side again, lord of the Scyldings, as you once had from him, the bane of the warriors' lives.

Then the gilded hilt was given to that old leader, the white-haired hero; that which was wrought by the giants of old was laid in his hands. So did it pass into the possession of the Danish king after the devils' downfall. It was the work of a wondrous smith, and now that the world was rid of that black-hearted fiend—the enemy of God, stained with murder—along with his mother, it now passed into the power of the people's king, best of all among the oceans who had ever distributed gold in Scandian lands.

Hrothgar spoke; he looked at the hilt, ancient relic, whereupon was etched the origin of that primeval conflict when the flood and rushing oceans destroyed the race of giants. Their fate was fearful; they were a race estranged from the Eternal God, who paid them final retribution in the ravaging waves. All around the hilt of shining gold Hrothgar saw, in runic verse, for whom the serpentine-ornamented sword, best among blades, was wrought in ancient days.

The wise son of Healfdene spoke, and all were silent: "Lo, he who is followed by so many folk as I am, and who remembers the times of old as I do, may say in truth as I say that this prince is of a noble breed! Thus exalted, your fame, oh Beowulf my friend, will spread on fleet wings, far and wide over the realms of many folk. Nevertheless, you carry your might with modesty and wisdom. I pledge you my love, as I promised you formerly; you are destined to prove a sure and lasting comfort to your thanes, and a bastion to all your warriors.

"Heremod, offspring of Ecgwela of the honorable Scyldings, was not this way. He grew strong not for their pleasure, but for mortal combat and for deathblows against the Danish people. Enraged, he crushed his comrades who sat with him at the mead-hall! So he went forth alone, the illustrious chieftain, far from human society—even though the mighty God had exalted him above all men by endowing him with the attractions of strength and courage. Nevertheless, his mind became bloodthirsty in its passions, and his hoard grew—for he did not give rings to the Danes who merited them. He endured all joyless, and suffered in woe as his people were estranged from him.

"Find in this your lesson, and be advised of what is virtuous! I have spoken this verse to you from the wisdom of many bygone winters.

"It is wondrous to tell how the mighty God in the strength of his spirit sends wisdom to mankind and grants position and authority—he holds dominion over everything. Betimes, He allows the heart of a nobly-born hero to turn towards dominion, and gives him earthly joy in his ancestral throne; He gives him regions of the world that are so extensive and massive that in all his wisdom he cannot fathom the ends of it. And so he grows in wealth, and neither illness nor age can harm him. No burdensome worries overshadow his heart, and no sword of hatred held by the enemy ever threatens him. The wide world bends to his will, and no one opposes it."

CHAPTER 25 X X V

"UNTIL AT LAST, overweening pride grows and develops within him, and the soul-warden slumbers; that which controls his might sleeps too strongly, and the assassin draws nigh, secretly shooting shafts from his bow! Then is he, the helmeted man, struck in his heart by the sharpest arrow; he cannot defend himself from the wiles of the hellish spirit. He fancies that what he has long possessed is too little. Covetous and hateful, he sees no glory in the giving of rings for his fame. He forgets and spurns what the consequences would be, and lightly esteems all that God, the Wielder of Wonder, has given him of wealth and glory. Yet in the end, it happens, as always, that the fragile body yields and falls to its fate, and another comes—one who joyously distributes treasure of the king's old hoard with no thought of his forbearer's ways.

"Drive such evil thoughts from you, dear Beowulf, most excellent youth! Choose for yourself a better course of eternal profit, and do not tend toward arrogance, famed warrior! Your might is in bloom for only a while, but before long sickness or sword shall diminish your strength, either by the fire's fangs or the waves of a flood; by the bite of a blade or a wielded spear; by age or by the darkening of your eyes' clear beam. Death will suddenly take even you, oh hero of war!

"Just so did I rule the Ring-Danes during half a hundred years, holding sway beneath the heavens, and bravely did I shield them from many mighty nations of the whole earth until it seemed to me that I could find no foe under the expanse of the sky. Lo, then came a sudden shift! On my secure throne was joy traded for grief when Grendel, that infernal foe, began to raid my home; those ruthless raids made me heavy in heart, and I suffered much unrest. Praise be to God, the Eternal Lord, that I have lived so long that, after evil has lasted so long, my eyes could gaze upon his hewn and bloody head!

"Go now to the mead-bench! Be glad at the banquet, worthy warrior! At the morrow's dawn a wealth of treasure will be dealt between us."

The Geats' lord was glad, seeking quickly to take his seat as the wise king commanded him. Then, as before, a fair banquet was served afresh to the company in the hall, those famous warriors.

The helm of night grew dark over the band of drinkers. The mighty ones rose, for the white-haired one, the aged Scylding, wanted to hasten to his rest. The Geat, that stalwart shield-fighter, also yearned for sleep. Now weary of wandering, the honored warrior from afar was led forth by a chamberlain, a thane who by custom would care for all such needs as adventuring warriors were likely to have in those days of yore.

And so the stout-hearted hero rested. The hall's royal golden gables rose high in the air. The guest slept on until a black raven heralded heaven's glory with a merry heart. Then bright light came streaming over the shadows. The swordsmen hastened, and all the princes were eager to go forth to their homes; the great-hearted guest would guide his keel on a voyage far from there.

The stalwart one then bid that Hrunting be brought to the son of Ecglaf and then had him take that excellent weapon. He gave thanks for the use of it and said that he reckoned it a great help in battle, a war-friend most beloved. He did not speak ill of the blade's edge—he was a noble-hearted man!

Now eager to depart and equipped in arms, the warriors waited while he who was honored by the Danes went to his host. The mighty prince hastened to the throne and greeted Hrothgar.

C H A P T E R X X V I

BEOWULF, SON OF Ecgtheow, spoke: "Lo, we seafarers who have come from afar would say that we now want to go to Hygelac. We have here been hosted to our heart's content; you have been very generous to us. If I am able to win more of your love and gratitude, oh lord of men, through works of war upon the earth beyond what I have done, I am still quite ready! If word comes to me from across the seas that your neighbors raid and alarm you, as those who hated you have previously done, then I will bring a thousand thanes, all heroes, to help you. I know that Hygelac, defender of his folk, though his years be few, will give me aid by word and deed to serve you, wielding a forest of spears to win your triumph and lend you strength when you lack men. If your Hrethric, son of a king, should come to the Geats' court, he will surely find his friends there. Each man who thinks himself brave should visit a far-off land."

In answer, Hrothgar spoke: "The wisest God has sent these words of yours to your soul! Never have I heard such sage counsel from one so young in years. You are strong in might, wise in understanding, and careful in speech. I deem it likely that if ever Hrethel's heir, your elder and lord, be taken by a spear and the grim sword of battle, or the people's leader by illness or iron—and if your life remains—the Sea-Geats will find no more fitting man to choose as their chieftain and king, as a guardian of the heroes' hoard, if you want to keep your kinsman's kingdom! Your disposition is more and more pleasing to me, beloved Beowulf! You have brought about mutual peace between both our peoples, the Geats and the Spear-Danes, so that we will refrain from murderous strife and war such as we once waged. As long as I rule this wide realm, let our treasure troves be as one. Let heroes greet one another with gold over the seas where fishes bathe, and let the ringéd prow bear tokens of affection over the ocean's waves. I know my people are constant in mind towards both friend and foe, and they keep honor such as it was kept in olden days."

That shelterer of warriors, Healfdene's son, give into his trust twelve more treasures, and bid him go with those gifts to visit his beloved people, arriving well and returning soon. The renowned king of kin, the Scyldings' chieftain, then kissed that peerless thane and clasped him by the neck. The white-haired one's tears flowed quickly. Two paths did he who was heavy with winters foresee, but one seemed more likely: that they should never look upon one another again, and he would never hear him in the hall. This hero was so dear to him that he sought to stifle his breast's sobs in vain, and the deep affections of his soul were lodged in his thoughts as they flowed in his blood.

Then Beowulf, a happy warrior glad of his golden gifts, went over the grassy plain. The wave-wanderer was riding at anchor as it awaited its owner. As they hastened onward, they praised Hrothgar's generosity—he was a king without peer, blameless in every way until age, which spares no mortal, had broken his glorious might.

CHAPTER XXVII

NOW THE STALWART and ever-courageous thanes came to the ocean; they wore ringmail, those woven war-vests. The watchman, trustworthy as ever, noted the prince's return. No words of suspicion came from the cliff-peaks when he rode forth to greet them. He called "Welcome!" to the Geats, as the warriors in shining armor marched toward their ship. Then from the beach was their spacious, ring-prowed ship loaded to the brim with steeds, treasure, and armor; its mast rose high over the wealth from Hrothgar's hoard.

Beowulf presented to the boat-warden a sword bound with gold, and ever after was he more respected on the mead-bench for owning that blade, the ancient heirloom. After boarding their ocean-keel, they drove through the deep and left Daneland. Then a sea-cloth was set up—a sail was made firm to the mast with ropes—and the sea-timbers creaked. The wind rushing over the waves did not lead the wave-swimmer off her course, but the craft sped on; with foaméd neck did it float forth over the waves. Their elegant prow sailed over the briny currents until they sighted the Geatish cliffs, those familiar headlands. Driven by the winds, the boat rode up high upon the beach. The harbor-guard stood ready to help at the haven; he had already spied the craft from afar long before and awaited those beloved men there. He bound the broad-bosomed boat fast with anchor-cables, lest the ocean's billows tear away that trustworthy timber. Then Beowulf had them unload the treasure, the gold and jewels; it was no great journey from there to the ring-giver, Hygelac son of Hrethel. That majestic king and his clan dwelt close by the sea-wall; the building was lofty, with the king in his high hall.

Hygd was quite young, but wise and discreet. Although the daughter of Hæreth had spent only a few winters in the fortress, she had found a home; she was neither mean-spirited nor grudging in giving gifts to the Geatish thanes. She did not show the pride of Thyrth, that famous queen of the people whose savagery was terrible. None of the dear liegemen (save her lord alone) were so bold that they would dare to look the lady full in the face, lest they find that iron chains of death be their lot! And, shortly after he had been seized, his doom would be decreed—a burnished blade would make an evil murder. This is no way for a queen to be, for a lady to practice. Although she is without peer, no wife should, upon false pretense of injury, take the life of a warrior thane! But Hemming's kinsman put this in check; men then told over their cups of ale that she wrought fewer thane-deaths and acts of vengeance after she was sent as a gold-adorned bride to the young champion who was noble and brave, that vaunted prince Offa. Sent to his hall over the fallow sea-fields at her father's bidding, there she has ever since been known for her kindness as she, throned in royalty and rich in wealth, used her fate well and was well-loved by the king of warriors. He, among all the heroes I have ever heard tell of, from sea to sea, seemed most excellent among the sons of men. Hence Offa was praised by far-off men for his feats of war and grace, and that warrior bold with his spear ruled wisely over his home kingdom. Eomær, the aid to the heroes, was born to him. He was Hemming's kinsman, grandson of Garmund, and skilled at war.

CHAPTER 28 XXVIII

THE STALWART ONE hastened with his companions; he treaded along the wide strands of sandy seashores. The world's great candle, the sun, shone from the south. With mighty steps did they stride along to the place where they knew that the young and brave war-king, shelter-of-warriors and slayer of Ongentheow, shared his rings within the fortress.

To Hygelac was Beowulf's coming promptly told: that clansman, his shield-companion, was alive and well, coming to the court from the battle-games, marching homeward. As the king commanded, room for the roamers was quickly made within the hall.

He who had come safe from battle sat by his sovereign; kinsman sat by kinsman, and the kind lord greeted his loyal man with gracious words. Hæreth's daughter came through the high hall dispensing mead; she who was winsome to the warriors took the wine-cup into the heroes' hands.

Hygelac then questioned his companion carefully in that lofty hall; he deeply longed to know how the adventures of the Sea-Geats had gone. "How fared your quest, beloved Beowulf, when your questing swept you there over the briny sea to seek battle and combat at Heorot? Did you at all aid Hrothgar, the honored chieftain, in his wide-known woes? My sad heart seethed with waves of care, and I mistrusted the adventure for so dear a man; I long begged you not seek that slaughtering monster at all, but to allow the South-Danes to settle their feud with Grendel themselves. I thank God that I have now been allowed to see you safe and sound!"

Beowulf, son of Ecgtheow, spoke: "It is no secret, Hygelac my lord; the deadly struggle between Grendel and me is known to many men. We fought upon that field where he had surely wrought too many sorrows upon the conquering Scyldings—unending evils. I avenged all these; because of the tumult at dawn, nobody in the whole of Grendel's breed, the loathsome race that has long lived in the fens, can boast.

"I first went to greet Hrothgar in his ring-hall, where Healfdene's kinsman promptly assigned me a seat by his son and heir once my purpose was made plain to him. The company was joyous; never in my life have I heard under heaven's vault such merriment of men over mead in the hall! The noble queen, the pledge of peace between nations, cheered the young clansmen by giving golden clasps to various ones before she sought her seat. Hrothgar's daughter betimes carried the ale-cup to the princes in turn—I heard these hall-companions say when she offered carvings of gold to the warriors that her name was Freawaru. The gold-adorned maiden is pledged to the merry son of Froda. This seems sagacious to the keeper of the kingdom, that friend of the Scyldings: he deems it wise to wed the woman and ward off a massive blood-feud. But seldom does the slaughtering spear sleep for long, even though the bride is fair!

"The Heathobard lord will not well like it when he and all his liegemen see a Danish thane in that stalwart crowd accompany the lady in their hall, and upon him the ancient heirlooms gleam; hard and ring-covered, they are Heathobard's treasure—weapons that they once wielded well until they lost loyal liegemen and their own lives in the game of battle. Then, while drinking ale, some old spear-fighter will gaze upon this heirloom and think of spear-brought death—he is somber and his heart is heavy— and he tries the temper and prods the soul of the young hero, awakening war-hate with words like these:

" 'Can't you, my comrade, recognize that sword which your father carried in his final battle while wearing his helmet, when the Danes killed him, and the stout Scyldings took the field after the carnage and Withergild's death? Now, the son of one of those murdering Danes, proud of the loot, walks into our hall and boasts of the slaughter; he's wearing the treasure which you by right ought to own!'

"So he urges and goads him at every turn with galling words until the time comes that Freawaru's thane must sleep in his blood, losing his life to sword-bite for his father's deed. But the liegeman flies away, alive, to the land he knows. And thus the princes' oaths on both sides would be broken when Ingeld's breast swells with war-hatred, and the love for his wife grows cooler after those billows of care. So I do not highly esteem the

Heathobard's loyalty, nor do I deem their alliance with the Danes sincere or their friendship firm.

"But I return now to tell of Grendel, O giver of treasure, and fully tell how the hand-combat of heroes ended. When the jewel of heaven had fled far over the fields, the fierce monster came, savage foe of the night, to seek us out where we guarded the hall in safety and security. The raid was deadly to Hondscio; he was doomed to die there. That armored warrior was first to be killed. Grendel set his murderous mouth upon our mighty kinsman and devoured the brave man's entire body.

"But even so, the murderous assassin with bloody fangs appeared unready to leave that golden hall empty-handed; confident of his strength, he attacked me and grasped me with greedy hands. On him hung a wide and marvelous satchel, wound round about with cords and skillfully wrought with demonic craft of dragon's hides. The fiendish foe wanted to thrust me, an innocent man, inside there along with many others. He did not do so when I stood upright in rage. It would take too long to relate how I repaid in full that land-ravager for his cruel deeds, but this people of yours, my prince, gained fame there by my fighting. He escaped and got away, preserving for a little while his life, but his stronger hand stayed behind him in Heorot; in abject spirits did that outlaw fall at the lake bottom.

"For this struggle did the Scyldings' friend pay me upon the morn with much beaten gold and many treasures. We all sat at the banquet tables, and there was song and mirth. A gray-haired Scylding told tales from the days of yore. While the hero awakened his harp, that delightful wood, he chanted ballads of truth and sadness, or the magnanimous king would recount a legend of wonder. At times, one now chained with age would yearn for the battles of old in his youth; the white-haired fellow's heart would well up within him as this one wise in winters would revive memories. Thus did we feast in the hall at our leisure the whole day until another night fell over the earth.

"Then, ready and eager for vengeance, Grendel's mother set woefully forth. Her son was dead by the war-hate of the Geats; now this monstrous women slew a foe in her fury to avenge her offspring. Life departed from old Æschere, the loyal counselor. When morning broke, those Danish people could do nothing for him; they could not consume the lifeless man with flame and set the man they mourned upon the funeral pyre, for she had carried the corpse in her cruel claws beneath the mountain stream. Of all the griefs that had long beset the lord of his folk, this was the most bitter for Hrothgar. The leader, sad in his soul, then beseeched me—by your leave—to hazard life in the rush of waters, thereby testing valor and gaining renown. He pledged me compensation. It is widely known that I then found that savage guardian of the lake bottom in the waters. There we wrestled in hand-to-hand combat for a while; the waves welled with blood, and in that briny hall I hewed the head from Grendel's mother with a stout blade—thereby gaining my life, though not without danger. My doom had not yet come. Then that haven for heroes, Healfdene's son, gave me plentiful and valuable gifts as a reward.

CHAPTERS XXIX - XXXI

"SO DID THIS king hold to the old customs such that I lacked nothing in the rewards I gained, those requitals for my achievement. Healfdene's heir gave me gifts to use as I thought suitable. Now to you, my king, I offer them all and gladly give them. I find favor in your grace alone. I have few good kinsmen besides you, Hygelac!"

Then he commanded them to carry in the standard with the boar's head, the high battle-helmet, the gray coat of mail, and the splendid sword. He then spoke in this way: "To me did the wise old king, Hrothgar, give this battle gear, and with these gifts he added that the story of them be promptly told to you. For a while, Heorogar the king held it; he was lord of the Scyldings' lands for a long time. Yet this sovereign did not leave it, this battle-jacket, to his son, the bold Heoroweard—dear as he was to him. Treasure it well!"

I also heard that close upon the footsteps of this treasure followed four steeds, each like the other; he presented the treasures and horses to the king. In this way should kinsmen act—not weaving a net of wiles for one another or secretly contriving treacherous death for one's neighbor and comrade. The nephew of Hygelac, bold in battle, was always true to him, and each kept watch over the other's welfare.

I heard as well that he presented to Hygd the necklace, the wonderfully wrought treasure given to him by Wealtheow, the king's daughter, along with three elegant and saddled steeds. From then on the queen's breast was decorated with this bright treasure.

So did Ecgtheow's son gain renown in acts of valor and mighty deeds.

He never killed comrades or kin at the ale-cup, and his mood was never cruel, although among the sons of earth his strength was greatest—a gift sent by God to that excellent leader, who used it in prudence. He was long spurned and thought worthless by the Geatish warriors, and at mead the clan's chieftain often failed to favor him at all. The strong men deemed him weak and an unpromising prince—but a reversal of all these insults came when the warrior was honored.

Then the bastion of the warriors, the king famed in battle, commanded Hrethel's gold-decorated heirloom to be brought within. No Geat ever knew a more noble prize in the shape of a sword. He laid this blade in Beowulf's lap, and assigned him seven thousand hides of land,[†] with a large house and a seat of authority. They both held lands and a homestead there by right of their inheritance, but the kingship went to the one because he was the elder.

Now with the passage of years, it happened that Hygelac perished in dread raids; Heardred, despite a wall of shields, was also hewn by swords at the forefront of his fighting men when the Scylfings, stalwart heroes, sought him and overwhelmed Hereric's nephew with arms.

And so it was that the kingship of that broad land came into Beowulf's hands, and he ruled it well for fifty winters. He was a venerable old king who protected his land, until on dark nights, one dragon began to rage. It guarded a hoard high upon a hill in a steep barrow of stone. A straight path led beneath the hill; it was seldom traveled by men. One man, however, chanced upon that cave and saw the heathen's hoard. While the watcher slept, he took in his hand a golden goblet and did not give it back. The guardian's wrath would soon make the prince and people pay for those thievish wiles!

CHAPTER 32 XXXII

HE WENT THAT way, to the dragon's den, not by his own will, but under dire threat of death. Out of deep necessity did that slave of some prince flee—from fear of deadly lashings; seeking shelter as a guilty man would, he entered inside. [But at the sights that guest did quail as fright seized him; yet, in despair, the fugitive regained his courage, taking the cup from the hoard before he fled in terror.] There was a goodly store of such ancient heirlooms in the earthen cavern, carefully hidden away by some old and long-forgotten prince in ancient times—those precious treasures were the legacy of a noble race. For death had driven them all hence, and he alone was left alive; the last one of his clan, he wept for his friends, yet wished to stay, and, even if only for a brief respite, guard the treasure, his one delight.

The barrow had recently been made ready near the shore; the ocean's waves were near, and it was nigh to the cliff, hidden and secured. There within did he place his royal heirlooms, and that guardian of treasure heaped the hoard high with weighty gold. He spoke a few words: "Hold now, oh earth, that which nobles have held, since heroes cannot! Lo! It was first from you that brave men took it! But death in battle cruelly seized and killed all my clansmen, robbing them of life and the joys of a liegeman. I have none left to lift the sword or cleanse the costly carvéd cup, the gleaming tankard. The valiant are departed. That hard helmet, inlaid all about with gold, shall shed its plating, for the polishers who could brighten and burnish the mask of battle now sleep. The battle armor that braved the bite of steel among the clash of shields now rusts with the bearer. No longer can that ringmail travel abroad at the hero's side with the famous chieftain! There is no delight of the harp, no gladness of the merry wood! No good hawk now flies through the hall! No fleet steeds stamp at the fortress entrance! Battle and death have bereaved my race of its flowers." Sorrowful in his mood, he groans his woes alone for them all and bitterly weeps day and night until death's fell waves rush over his heart.

The dazzling hoard was found standing exposed near that ancient evil one who haunts the burrows, blazing at twilight—the scaly dragonfiend, who flies by night robed in fire; the countryfolk hold him in awful dread. It is his fate to go to the hoard underground, where he passes many winters watching heathen gold; he gains nothing through this! This powerful bane of men thus held the hoard in the earthen house for three hundred winters—until one kindled wrath in his heart by taking that precious cup to the king and entreating him to grant him peace. So the barrow was plundered, and treasure was carried off. The plea of the wretched man was granted; that king saw for the first time that which was fashioned in days of long ago.

When the dragon awoke, this new quarrel was kindled. He immediately sniffed the scent along the stone. The dark-hearted one found the footprints of that foe who had walked undetected by the creature's head. So may a man not doomed elude death and exile, if only he gains the Maker's grace! The guardian of gold went tracking over the ground, eager to find the man who had brought mischief upon his slumber. Savage and burning, he circled 'round the barrow; no man was in that wasteland. Yet he desired war and was eager for combat. He entered and sought the cup, soon discovering that a mortal had sifted through his treasure, the noble gold. The treasure's guardian waited with difficulty until evening came; the barrow-keeper boiled with wrath and wished to pay his foe with flame for the loss of the precious cup. Now the day had fled, as the dragon wanted. It no longer remained by its wall, but, burning and robed in flame, he flew off. The beginning of this was fearful for the sons of earth, and it soon resulted in their lord's fate: a dreadful end.

CHAPTER XXXIII

THEN DID THE evil monster belch forth fire, and merry farmsteads burned; the light of the blaze glared high, frightening all the countrymen. That loathsome one, as it flew about, would leave no living thing. The dragon's war-making was seen everywhere; his fiendish rage was evident far and near as that fell destroyer hated and ravaged the Geatish people. At the hint of dawn, he hastened to his hidden lair. It had bathed the folk of the land in flame, with fire and coals. It trusted in its barrow, its warcraft, and its ramparts—that confidence was in vain!

This crushing woe was told to Beowulf the King swiftly and certainly; his own home, best of buildings and throne of gifts for the Geats, melted in the waves of flame. This was the heaviest of sorrows to the good old man, and he was sad at heart. The wise man assumed that he had angered his sovereign God, broken the ancient law, and embittered the Lord. Black thoughts welled within his mind, as was never his custom. The fiery dragon had destroyed by flame the folk's own fortress, that stronghold by the sea's shore; the warrior king, prince of the Geats, plotted vengeance. The shield-of-warriors, commander-of-the-princes, had them craft for him a wondrous war-shield made completely of iron; he well knew that the forest's wood was worthless against fire—linden could not help. The valorous prince was fated to end his allotted days on this earth, and the dragon with him—though it had long watched over the wealth of the hoard!

Then did that giver of rings think it shameful that he should pursue the far-flyer with a troop, a large host; he did not fear the battle, nor think the dragon's warcraft a threat to his might and valor—he had passed through many desperate ventures, perils of war, contests, and battle-clashes since the proud victor had purged Hrothgar's hall and killed Grendel's kin, that loathsome spawn, in a mighty grapple.

Not the least among these encounters was that hand-to-hand combat when Hygelac fell, and the lord of the Geatish folk, son of Hrethel, died by the thirsty sword in the rush of battle in Frisian lands; he was felled with the blade. From there did Beowulf flee through his might and swimming power, though alone. His arms were burdened with thirty coats of mail when he reached the sea! Nor yet did the Hetware,[†] who carried shields against him in the strife, have reason to boast of their warcraft—for few of them escaped the fight with the hero to seek their homes!

Ecgtheow's son, lonely and forlorn, sought his land, where Hygd offered him hoard and realm, treasure and a throne. She had no confidence that her son could save their kingdom from hostile hordes now that Hygelac was dead. But in no way could that bereaved people change the prince's mind and have him accept lordship over Heardred to be ruler of the realm; he upheld this youth and advised him honorably until he had grown older and reigned over the Storm-Geats.

Wandering exiles sought Heardred from across the seas: the sons of Ohtere who had spurned the rule of that Scylfings' crown, the best and bravest of those who gave rings in the Swedish lands—he was a noble hero of the sea-kings' lineage. Hence came Heardred's demise, for he gave those sons shelter, and death came to the son of Hygelac by the blade's fell blow. But Onela, son of Ongentheow, sought his house and home again once Heardred fell, leaving Beowulf as lord of the Geats and the master of the gift-throne. He was a good king!

CHAPTER XXXIV

H E CONTEMPLATED AVENGING his lord's death in later days; he became a friend to Eadgils when he was friendless. He supported the son of Ohtere with a force of weapons and warriors, sending them over the sea: he at length had his vengeance by means of this cold and painful exile when Eadgils slew Onela the king.

Thus did the son of Ecgtheow pass safely through many struggles; through dire perils with daring deeds did he come, until this day when his fight with the dragon doomed him. In rage, the lord of the Geats went with eleven comrades to seek the dragon. He had learned by then how all the harm and clan-killing had come about: that precious cup had been laid on the lap of the lord by the one who found it. In the company was a thirteenth man, the beginner of all these conflicts and ills. A captive burdened with woe, he was forced, cringing with reluctance, to lead them on until he came to that cavern and hall, the barrow, a cave near the surging ocean waves.

It was full of jewels and carven gold; a vigilant guardian held these treasures. This war-demon lurked within his lair, and the task of gaining entrance was not an easy one for any among mankind! The hero king sat on the headland; the gold-friend of the Geats spoke words of farewell to his hearth-companions. His soul was full of sorrow; it was troubled and doom-ridden. Fate stood well ready to greet this gray-haired man and to seize the treasure of his soul by sundering life from body. This warrior's spirit would not long be entwined with flesh.

Beowulf, son of Ecgtheow, spoke: "I labored through many battles in my youth, and fought many contests; I remember them all. I was seven winters old when the king of treasures, friend of his people, received me from my father; he held me and cared for me, did Hrethel the king, with food, money, and faithful kinship. He never treated me more poorly as a son in his fortress than those who were born to him: Herebeald, Haethcyn, and my lord Hygelac. The bed of death was made for the eldest of these in unnatural fate by a brother's deeds; Haethcyn laid my own dear liege low with an arrow, killing him with a bow made of horn. He missed his mark and shot down his mate—one brother killed the other with a bloody shaft. It was a fight without blood-price, a fearful sin; it was a horror to Hrethel, and yes, difficult though it was, the prince must die unavenged!

"Likewise, it is an awful thing for an aged man to endure for his young son to ride upon the gallows. He makes a lament, a dirge for his son hanging there for the ravens' benefit; the old, disabled man cannot rescue him now! Even so, at every daybreak, he is reminded of the heir who is now Elsewhere; he cares not to wait and see another son become the ward of his fortress' wealth, now that one has received the fate of death for his deeds.

"Forlorn, he sees his son's lodgings. It is a deserted mead-hall, and the wind sweeps through those chambers that are bereft of revel. The rider sleeps, and the hero is hidden in the grave; no harp resounds, and in the courts there is no mead-merriment as there once was.

"THEN HE GOES to his chamber and alone chants a dirge for his lost one. His homestead and house all seems too large. So did the crown of the Geats hide waves of woe within his heart. He could in no way avenge the foul slaughter upon the killer, nor could he even pursue the hero at all with loathing deeds, even though he did not love him. And because of the sorrow his soul endured, he gave up the gladness of men and chose the light of God. As the wealthy do, he left lands and cities to his sons when he went from the earth.

"There was conflict and battle between Swede and Geat over the oceans' expanse; war arose, the hard horrors of battle, and when Hrethel died, Ongentheow's sons became impetuous and bold. They brooked no peace treaty over the seas, but drove their boats to harass in hatred around Hreosnabeorh. My cousins had vengeance for that feud and outrageous wrong—this is well-known. One of them, however, paid for it with his heart's blood; it was a hard bargain. That fray proved fatal for Haethcyn, the first among the Geats. The murderer was killed at morning, I heard, and brother avenged brother with a swordstrike when Ongentheow engaged Eofor there. The war-crown was split wide, and the white-haired Scylfing fell down pale. The hand that struck him had made reckoning in many feuds, and did not flinch from forcing the fatal blow.

"I paid for the treasures that Hygelac gave me with war as I had the opportunity to do so with my gleaming sword; he entrusted me with land, a homestead, and a house. He had no need to seek help among the Gepidæ, or the Spear-Danes, or the Swedish realm—lesser warriors that he would buy with wages! I always fought in the forefront, alone in the vanguard—and thus shall I fight while I remain in this life and so long as will last this blade, which has often, both then and now, stood me in good stead, since with my valor Dæghrefn, champion of the Hugas,[†] was killed by my hand. Nor did he go back from there to the Frisian king with booty and breast-ornaments, but that brave prince, the bearer of the standard, fell slain in battle. He was not killed by blade, but his bones were broken and his heart was stilled by a war-grip. Now will the edge of the sword, my hand, and the hard blade contend for the hoard."

Beowulf spoke, and made a battle-boast, his last one of all: "I have survived many wars in my youth, and now I, the old defender of the people, will once again seek battle and accomplish mighty deeds, if that fell destroyer will come forth from his cavern to fight me!" Then he hailed all the helmeted heroes, greeting the dear liegemen who were his comrades in war for the last time. "I would carry neither weapon, nor sword against the serpent, if I knew how I could make good my boast with such an enemy, as I did in the day of Grendel. But I must now fear fire in this fight, and poisonous breath, and so I bring with me breastplate and shield. I will flee not even one footstep from the barrow's keeper. One fight upon this rampart shall end our war, as fate which is master of mankind will allow. I am bold in spirit, and so I forbear more boasts against this wingéd warrior. Now wait by the barrow, you in coats of mail and battle gear, to see which of the two of us will bear the wounds of this battle-rush better. Wait for the finish. This is not your fight, nor is it fitting for any but me alone to test my might against this monster here and achieve heroism. I shall win that wealth mightily, or war shall seize your king and lord with cruel killing!"

The sturdy champion then stood up with his shield. Beneath his helmet, his face was stern; he carried his war-gear near the rugged cliffs, and he trusted in the might of his single manhood—such is not the way of the coward! Soon that warrior king, who survived many battles and furious clashes with foes, spied a rocky arch by the wall; out of the arch, a stream broke from the barrow. The brook's surface was hot with fire. He could never hope to come near the hoard unharmed; he could not endure that passage because of the dragon's flame.

Then did that Storm-Geat prince force a word from his lungs, and he burst with rage; he stormed with a strong heart, and his clear cry resonated loudly beneath the gray rocks of the cliffs. The hoard-guardian heard a human voice, and his rage was kindled. There was no more pause for making peace agreements! First to come forth from the cave was that hot stench of combat: the poison breath of that foul worm. The stout lord of the Geats raised his shield against the hated one by the stone path; that coiled foe came courageously seeking strife. The stalwart king drew his sword—that ancient heirloom had no dull edge—and each of the two felt fearful of his foe, though their hearts were fierce. The warrior king stood resolutely with his shield raised high, and the worm now coiled himself together; the mailed one waited.

That blazing serpent, curved like an arch, advanced upon him, gliding headlong and quickly. The shield protected the soul and body of the hero king for a time shorter than he would have desired; he had supposed that morning that he would achieve glory in combat. But Fate denied him the honors of victory. The lord of the Geats lifted his arm and struck the dire foe with the prince's heirloom. Its burnished edge was turned aside on the bone, and it bit more feebly than its noble master needed at that time in his time of duress. Then after the mighty blow, the barrow's keeper became furious with rage, and those vicious fires flew far and wide. The Geats' lord could not boast in the victor's glory—his sword had failed as it never should have, that renowned iron, and he was naked in combat! It was not an easy path for Ecgtheow's honored heir to tread over the plains as he won himself a home Elsewhere, as all men must do when they resign their allotted days.

It was not long before those champions closed ranks again. The hoard-guardian rallied his courage; he drew breath into his breast as he began once more, and the ruler of the people was hard-pressed in peril as he was encompassed with fire. Alas, for his band of comrades, the sons of princes, did not stand armed about him with a battle-stance, but they ran off to the woods to save their lives. But one soul was burdened with care, for true kinship can never be marred in a noble mind!

C H A P T E R X X X V I

IS NAME WAS Wiglaf, Weohstan's son, a beloved warrior and thane of the Scylding lord, a kinsman of Ælfhere. He now saw his king hard-pressed by the heat beneath his helmet. He brought to mind the prizes his lord had given him: a wealthy seat of honor in the Wægmunding homestead and every right in society that his father owned. He did not hesitate, but seized the yellow linden of his shield and drew a sword, known among men as the ancient heirloom of Eanmund, son of Ohtere, who, when an exile killed Weohstan in battle, won for his kin the brightly burnished helm, a coat of ringmail, and an old sword of the giants. Onela yielded these to him as well: the armor of the warrior-thane and the brave gear of battle. Although a brother's son was slain, Onela spoke no word about a feud. Weohstan kept this war-gear many winters, until his son had grown old enough to earn his warrior's rank as his sire had. He then gave to him among the Geats that armor and armament of every sort, after which he went forth—an aged man—and passed from life.

The young liegeman was now bidden to share the shock of battle with his lord and leader. His courage did not melt, and his father's bequest did not grow weak in war. So did the worm find out when the foes met in battle! Wiglaf spoke, and his words were sagacious. Sad in spirit, he said to his companions: "I recall the time when we drank mead in the banquet hall and promised to our prince, our ring-giver, to give him recompense with the war-gear, with tempered swords and helmets, if need of this type would befall him! This is why he chose us from among his army to aid him now; he spurred us on to glory and gave us these treasures because he counted us skilled warriors with the spear and brave beneath our helms. Although our lord hoped to finish this hero's work for us alone and unhelped—this defender of the people who has gained for himself glory greater than any man for his deeds of daring!—now the day is come that our noble liege has need of stout warriors' might. Let us now be bold to help the hero while the flame about him glows grimly! For, with God as my witness, I would far more want the fire to seize these limbs of mine, along with my lord, than to idle! It would be unfitting for us to bear our shields homeward lest we undertake to fell the foe and defend our Geat-lord's life. I know that it is not the way of loyalty in the days of old that the king alone among the Geatish warriors should endure and die in the fight! My sword and helm, breastplate and shield, shall serve our lord, though a common death overtake us both."

Then he strode through the deadly reek to aid his chieftain. He bore his helm of battle, and spoke a few words: "Dearest Beowulf, now make brave that boast of yours in your days of youth, that while your life should last, you would in no way let your glory decline! Now, steadfast prince, great in deeds, shield your life with all your strength! I will stand and help you."

At these words, the worm came on in fury; the murderous monster came for a second time with flame-billows flashing to seek its foes, those hated men. It burned the shield to the boss, and the breastplate failed to shelter the young spear-thane at all—yet the young warrior went quickly beneath his kinsman's shield, now that his own had been burned by the blaze. The bold king once again thought of glory, and with great might he drove his glaive into the dragon's head; this blow was given force by hate. But Nægling was splintered; Beowulf's blade, though ancient and gray, was broken in battle. It was not granted to him that the edge of iron should ever help him in battle—his hand was too strong, so the tales tell, and he tried to strike too hard with his strength, such that no matter whatsoever the strength of the swords he wielded, he was none the better for it.

Then for the third time the monstrous destroyer, the infuriated dragon of dread fire, rushed at the hero, who had yielded ground. Burning with baleful battle, its bitter teeth enclosed upon his neck, covering him with waves of blood that welled from his breast.

CHAPTER 37 XXXVII

I T IS NOW, men tell, that the young noble made known his nature—his enduring courage and his prowess—in his sovereign's need. Heedless of harm, he helped his kinsman with a stout heart though his hand was burned. He struck the loathsome monster a little lower; his bright and burnished sword penetrated; the beast's blaze began to dwindle.

The king at last recovered his wits and drew his war-knife, a biting blade hanging by his breastplate. The Geats' crown split that worm asunder, felling the foe. They had defeated the foe together, the two kinsmen—twin princes; so should a liegeman be in days of danger! This hour of conquest was the last of the king's valorous deeds, of his work in the world.

The wound which the earth-dragon had inflicted began to swell and flare up, and he soon found his chest boiling, as venom worked itself in deeply with evil. The prince, wise in his thoughts, walked on to the rock wall and sat staring at the structure of giants where the stone arch and the sturdy column stood forever in that earthen hall. There did the hand of the peerless liegeman wash his winsome lord with water. Covered with blood, the king and conqueror undid his helmet; the battle had wearied him. Despite his pain and mortal wound, Beowulf spoke; he knew full well that his portion of earthly bliss was done and gone, that the tale of his days had fled, and that death was near: "I would have given this armor to my son, if any heir would have come after me of my rightful blood. I ruled this people for fifty winters. There was no king of the neighboring clans, none at all, who would bring war-mates against me and threaten me with horrors. I observed social custom in my home, and cared for my own with justice. I did not seek feuds, nor have I falsely sworn any oath. Though I am fatally wounded, I am comforted by these, for the Ruler-of-Men will not seize me in wrath when my life must flee far from this mortal frame, for I did not kill my kinsmen!

"Now go quickly and gaze upon the hoard beneath the white rocks, beloved Wiglaf, now that the worm lies low in sleep—heartsick at his stolen spoil. And go in haste. I would behold the magnificent treasures, the store of gold, and have joy in the jewels and gems; I would resign the life and lordship I have long held with more ease when I look upon this splendid hoard."

C H A P T E R X X X V I I I

I THEN HEARD tell that the son of Weohstan went swiftly beneath the barrow's roof at the word and wish of his wounded king, the war-sick warrior; he bore his woven coat of mail and battle-vest. Then the victorious clansman, true and courageous, saw heaps of jewels and glistening gold on the ground as he went along that stone bench. There were wondrous things in the den of the dragon, dawn-flyer of old: many vessels and the unburnished bowls of bygone men, all encrusted; rusty helms from the days of old; and many arm-bands of wondrous weave. Such wealth of gold, booty from the barrow, can easily burden any human with pride—let him who will, heed it! His glance also fell upon a banner woven with gold, brilliantly embroidered with the noblest handiwork; its gleam was so bright that he could easily see the earthen floor and the other treasures. No trace of the serpent could be seen—the war-knife had dispatched him.

Then I heard that a single man emptied the hill of its hoard of giant-craft. He gathered to his breast cups and platters of his own choice, and he also took the ensign, that brightest of beacons. The iron edge of his lord's blade had deeply injured the one that guarded the golden hoard. For many years had it spread its hot and murderous fires 'round the barrow in billows of horror at the midnight hour, until it met its doom. The herald hastened and, burdened with spoil, retraced his steps. He was troubled with doubts in his brave soul about whether he'd find the lord of the Geats alive where he'd left him—by the cave's wall, quickly weakening. Then, carrying the treasures, he found his lord and king bleeding; that famous chief was at the extremity of life. The liegemen washed the king with water again; the tip of a word broke through the breast-treasures. Beowulf spoke, as he stared at the gold, sagely and sadly:

"I give thanks to my God, to the Wielder-of-Wonders, for the gold and treasure upon which I now gaze; I thank Heaven's Lord that I have been given grace to acquire such for my people ere the day of my death has come! Now have I bartered the last of my life for the hoard of treasure, so look well to the needs of my land! I shall not tarry any longer. Bid those warriors raise a cairn for my ashes. It will shine by the shores of the sea, and be a fair memorial lifted high to my folk on Hronës Headland. Seafarers may hail Beowulf's Barrow as they drive their keels over the scowling waves on their return."

The valorous king unclasped a gold collar from his neck and gave it to his vassal, along with the bright golden helmet, breastplate, and ring. He bid the youthful thane use them in joy. "You are the last remnant of our race and of the Wægmunding name, for Fate has swept all of my line, those princes of glory, into the land of doom. I must follow them."

This word was the last one harbored in the heart of that wise old man before he chose the hot, consuming flames of the death pyre. His soul fled his breast to seek the saints' reward.

C H A P T E R   X X X I X

I T WAS A HARD happenstance for the young hero to look upon his beloved lord and to find him lying on the ground at the end of life; a sorrowful sight. But the slayer, that terrible earth-dragon, also lay empty of breath. It lay felled in the fight, and the coiled worm could no longer rule its treasure. The edge of iron had ended its days, the hard work of hammers sharpened in battle; that far-flyer had fallen to the ground near its hoard-chamber and been silenced by its wound. No longer did it whirl aloft in sport at midnight and make visible its merriment in the pride of its treasures, but he collapsed on earth by the handiwork of that hero-king.

However, as the tales tell me, truly few among men achieve—though they be stalwart and sturdy. Be he ever so daring in valorous deeds, it is rare that he perils the poisonous breath of a foe or braves to rush upon the ring-hall when the warden keeps wakeful watch in the barrow. Beowulf paid the price of death for that precious hoard, and both of the combatants had found an end of this fleeting life.

Before long, those laggards in battle left the wood, those faint-hearted traitors, ten in all, who feared to brandish spears in their sovereign lord's sore distress. Now they carried their shields in shame and took the armor of battle to where the old man lay dead; then they gazed upon Wiglaf.

He sat, wearied, at the sovereign's shoulder; the good shieldsman tried to wake his lord with water. It did not in any way avail. Though he wished well, he could not keep the life of the battle-leader on earth, nor thwart the will of the Almighty God. The judgment of the Lord was law upon the deeds of every man then, just as it is now. The youth had a grim answer ready for those who had failed in courage. Wiglaf spoke, the son of Weohstan, and looked sadly upon those men he no longer loved:

"One can say truly indeed that the ruler who gave you golden rings and the war-gear in which you stand—for he oftentimes bestowed on the folk of his hall helm and breastplates at the ale-bench; the lord gave the liegemen the most trustworthy gear, both near and far, that he could find to give—that he wasted this battle-armor on men who failed when the foes came! The king could not at all venture to boast of his comrades in arms, although the Wielder of Victory, God, gave him such grace that he gained vengeance alone with his sword in his distress and need. I could afford him little protection in the struggle, but attempted nevertheless to do what I could not and help my kinsman. Its strength seemed ever to wane when I struck that fatal foe with a weapon, and the fire flowed less strongly from its head. Too few were the heroes who thronged to our king when the dire contest overtook him! Now must the giving of treasure, the presentation of swords, and the joys of homes and wealth, depart from you. All will you lose when highborn lords from afar hear of your flight and ignoble deeds. Verily, death is better for warriors than an entire life of shame!"

C H A P T E R   X L

HE THEN GAVE orders to announce the combat's conclusion at the
castle, that fortress on the cliff, where all the princes sat mourning and full of sorrow. They had been sitting by their shields all
morning, wondering whether they would wail in death or welcome home
their beloved lord. Nothing of the new tidings was held back, but the herald who rode up the headland told them everything: "Now the bounteous
chief of the Geatish folk lies on his deathbed; he dwells in the sleep of
slaughter by the serpent's deed! Beside him in like manner lies his mortal
foe, stricken with dagger-wounds; no sword would avail to work a wound
upon that awesome thing in any way. There sits Wiglaf, Weohstan's son, by
Beowulf's side, the living prince by the dead one, and he keeps an honor-
guard over friend and foe with a heavy heart.

"Now might our people look for warfare soon when once news of
the king's demise spreads afar to Frisian and Frank.[†] The strife with the
Hugas came when Hygelac fell as he fared with an embarked fleet upon
the Frisian lands, and the Hetware humbled him in war. They struck
with prowess and power overwhelming, so that the armored warrior was
forced to bow his head. That king could in no way give us treasure; he
was felled in the fight! Since that time has the Merowings'[†] favor failed us
completely.

"Nor do I in any way expect peace or truce from the Swedish folk—
indeed, it was a famous story, how Ongentheow took hope and life from
Hæthcyn son of Hrethel at Ravenswood, when the Geatish folk first sought
the war-like Scylfings in wanton pride. Soon that sage old father of Ohtere,

ancient and awful, delivered his onslaught and demolished the sea-king. He rescued the wife of his youth, mother of Onela and Ohthere, although he plundered her of gold. He then followed the foes who fled before him; sorely pressed and bereaved of their lord, they stole away to Ravenswood. With his army did he besiege there what swords remained, the weary and the wounded. He threatened woes the whole night long to the hard-pressed throng: some would his sword kill in the morning; some would go to the gallows-tree to please the ravens.

"But rescue came with the dawn of day to these desperate men when they heard the horn of Hygelac sound; with the sound of his trumpet, the brave king came, following their trail with the best of his thanes.

C H A P T E R   X L I

"THE GORY TRACK of the Swedes and Geats and the storm of their strife were seen from afar; each folk had revived the feud. The ancient king sought his citadel with his band of princes; he had much sorrow, and Ongentheow went up to his castle. He had tested Hygelac's war-craft, the prowess of that proud one, and would not test it again. He no longer defied those wandering warriors, and did not hope to save his hoard, son, and bride from the seamen: so the old king retired behind his earthen walls. Yet Swedes bearing the standards of Hygelac came after him, advancing proudly over peaceful plains, until the Hrethelings fought within the garrison. Then Ongentheow was held at bay with the edge of the sword; the white-bearded king of the people was forced to suffer Eofor's rage.

"In wrath, Wulf Wonreding struck the king with his weapon, and the chieftain's blood flowed in streams beneath his hair from that blow. The stout old Scylfing felt no fear, but directly repaid that bitter strike with better blows, once the king had collected himself. Wulf, the son of Wonred, was not swift enough to give answer to the aged king; the helm on Wulf's head was split in twain, and he bowed to the earth drenched in blood. He fell down but was not yet doomed; he later recovered, although the wound brought him close to death. Then did Eofor, thane of Hygelac, break through the wall of shields with his broad blade; his giant's sword crashed through the shield and helm. The king fell crouching; the old shepherd of the people was fatally wounded. There were many who bound the brother Wulf's wounds and lifted him up as fast as fate allowed them to take the field. But Eofor took from Ongentheow, one prince from the other, the iron breastplate, the hard hilted sword, and the helmet, carrying the white-haired king's gear to Hygelac. He accepted the spoils, and promised reward amidst the thanes—and, truly, he fulfilled it. When he came home, the Geatish lord, Hrethel's offspring, gave to Eofor and Wulf a wealth of treasure for that dire battle. Each of them received a hundred thousand in land and linked rings, and no men upon earth could estimate these mighty deeds at a lesser price! And upon Eofur he bestowed his only daughter, the pride of his home, as a pledge of loyalty.

"And so is the feud and the foeman's grudge, the enmity of men; I deem it sure that the Swedish people will attack us when once they learn that our leader of war, who ever defended land and hoard from all his foes, lies dead; he increased the welfare of his folk and remained a stalwart hero to the end. Haste is best now, when we go to look upon our Geatish lord and bear our bountiful ring-giver to the funeral pyre. It is not fitting that a trifle should burn with the noble man; but there is a hoard of precious gems and untold amounts of gold that were bought with a terrible price—he purchased the treasure with the last of his life. All of these must the fire devour and the flames envelop. No warrior must carry a jewel in memorial, nor fair maidens adorn her neck with a noble collar; nay, she will often pass over the paths of exile in sadness of spirit, stripped of her gold. Now the leader of our army has forsworn all laughter, game, and glee. Many a spear shall be clasped in hand in the morning's cold, and the lilt of the harp shall not wake these warriors, but the bleak raven shall flutter over the fallen, and he will boast to the eagle how bravely he ate when he and the wolf stripped the slain."

Thus did the ardent man tell sorrowful tidings, and he erred little in words or deeds. The dolorous warriors stood and climbed the Eagle's Crag; as they viewed the wondrous sight, their eyes welled with tears. There on the sand, they found their lifeless lord; the man who had given them rings in times of old was lying helplessly on his bed of sand. The final day had come to the valiant; death had seized the Weders' king in woeful slaughter.

They saw there as well the strangest thing lying prone near their leader on the field: the flying fire-drake, fearsome and grisly fiend, all scorched with flames. It was fifty foot-measurements in length where it lay. It had been supreme when it went aloft during the night-hours, then returning back to seek its den—now in death's fast clutches it had ended its joy in the earthen caverns. Nearby it stood pots and bowls; dishes lay about, and costly swords that were eaten with rust while they lay resting on the earth's lap for a thousand winters—for that entire large heritage, the gold of bygone men, was bound by enchantment, such that the hall's treasure might not be touched by any among mankind—save that one whom Heaven's King, God Himself, might grant the man of His choosing to open the hoard—even such a man as seemed fitting to Him.

CHAPTER XLII

IT PROVED A PERILOUS path for the man who had heinously hidden within that hall and walked there among the wealth beneath the walls. The watcher had killed that one and a few others, and the feud was avenged in furious fashion. A brave warrior should finish the end of his life with heroic deeds, when once the warrior can no longer live in the mead-hall with loving friends. Such was Beowulf's lot when he sought and fought the guardian of the barrow; he himself knew not in what way he was destined to leave the world at last. The potent princes who had deposited the gold had uttered a deep curse to last until doomsday, so that the man who invaded that ground to rob their hoard should be marked a criminal, hedged about with horrors, held by hell-bands, and racked with plagues. Yet it was not greed for gold, but heaven's grace that the king had ever kept in view.

Wiglaf, son of Weohstan, spoke: "Often must many warriors suffer much sorrow by the mandate of one, and so it has happened to us. The shepherd of our people, our beloved king, did not show care for our counsel when we urged him not to fight with the guardian of the gold, but to let him lie where he had long been—waiting in his earthen hall and awaiting the end of the world and the judgment of heaven. This hoard is ours, but it has been dearly won—the fate that carried Beowulf, our king and lord, was dire. I was inside there, and I viewed all of the treasures in the chamber, inasmuch as my path underneath the earthen walls was opened for me by no gentle means. I eagerly seized a heap from that hoard, such as my hands could bear, and carried it quickly back to my liege and lord.

He was still alive and still wielded his wits. The wise old man said much in his death-pangs; he had me send you greetings and bade that, when he breathed no more, you construct for him a high barrow on the place of his balefire—a mighty memorial. Among men, he was the most famous warrior throughout the wide earth, so long as he had the joy of his jewels and castle.

"Now let us hasten to see and search this store of treasure a second time, this spectacle beneath the earthen walls. I will show you the way so that you will have your fill of gazing upon golden collars and rings. Let the bier be ready and all in order when we come out, so to carry our king and commander to the place where he shall long abide, safe in the shelter of the sovereign God."

Then did the son of Weohstan command his brave warriors and ordered many of them who owned homesteads to bring firewood from afar for the famed-one's funeral. "Now must fire devour and scowling flames feed on the fearless warrior who often stood strong in the showers of iron as storms of arrows sped from the string, shot over the shield-wall; those shafts held firm as the feather-fittings eagerly followed the barb."

Thereupon did the sage young son of Weohstan choose seven of the chieftain's thanes, the best he found within the company, and with these warriors he was one of eight that went under the dangerous roof. One warrior bore a lighted torch in his hand and led the way. They cast no lots for the looting of the hoard, when once those warriors saw it lying there helpless and without a guardian in the hall. Little did any man mourn when they hastily hauled it out, that dearly bought treasure! They cast the dragon over the cliff for the waves to take, and the surges swallowed that guardian of gems. Then was woven gold loaded upon a wagon—it was countless in measure—and the king, that white-haired warrior, was borne on a bier to Hrónesness.

C H A P T E R   X L I I I

THE GEATISH FOLK constructed upon the earth a funeral pyre of no small dimensions, and hung it about with helmets, battle shields, and bright breastplates, as he requested. Amidst it they laid the illustrious chieftain, the hero and beloved lord. That hugest of balefires was then awakened on the hill by the warriors. Woodsmoke rose black over the blaze, and the roar of the flame shot upward as it mingled with the sound of weeping. The wind became still, and the heart of the fire's heat broke the frame of bones. With distressed hearts heavy-laden with care, they mourned their liege lord's death. Likewise, a dirge of sorrow [was sung for Beowulf by a woman; with hair braided up, she repeatedly said that she dreaded the evil days to come—days full of death, bloodshed, the horror of warriors, and captivity.] Heaven swallowed the smoke.

The Geatish folk fashioned a broad and high barrow on the headland, visible to seafarers abroad. In ten days, their toil had raised the beacon for him brave in battle. Around the brands of the pyre they built the worthiest wall that the wisest men could contrive with their wits. They placed in the barrow collars, rings, and such wealth as the stalwart heroes had lately captured in the hoard, trusting the ground with the treasure of princes, and placing the gold in the earth, where it lies, forever useless to men, as it was in days of old.

Then twelve sons of princes, warriors skilled in battle, rode around the barrow to make a lament, mourn their king, chant their dirge, and honor his name. They lauded his reign and praised his feats of prowess;

it is fitting that men should extol their liege lord with words and cherish him in love when the lord goes hence from life and take his departure from the home of his body.

Thus the men of Geatland, his hearth-companions, mourned their hero's passing, and said that of all the kings of the earth, he was the mildest and most belovéd of his men; kindest to his kin, and the most eager for praise.

GLOSSARY

PRELUDE

Danes–the residents of Denmark. Hrothgar, Hrothulf, and the Scylding dynasty of kings mentioned in *Beowulf* are actually spoken of in other Danish and Germanic sources (such as the poem *Widsith*). Some believe that Heorot, the hall of the Danes mentioned in Beowulf, was located on the island of Sjaelland, near the modern-day city of Roskilde, Denmark.

mead–The mead-hall was a fortress and gathering place for medieval Norse and Germanic tribes. Members of society could gather there in safety under the king or chieftain's protection so that they could feast, listen to or tell stories, and receive gifts from the king. It is interesting to note that *Valhalla* and *Folkvang*, two divine mead-halls from Scandinavian mythology, are the places where dead souls go in the afterlife. The mead-hall is the center of this society, and Grendel's attack on the hall is, therefore, an assault upon the fabric of society itself.

CHAPTER I
—

CHAPTER II

blood-gold–The act of paying "blood-gold" (*wergild*) was a method of forestalling vengeance in Scandinavian societies. If one man killed another, he or his family could pay money to the bereaved relatives to keep them from bringing death upon the original killer (and his relatives) in turn. The amount to be paid was generally dependent on the social rank of the individual who was killed. This was a method for ending the cycle of blood feuds that could (and did) ravage these societies.

CHAPTER III

Geats–According to the poem, the Geats are a seafaring tribe from the south of Sweden; they appear to have been conquered at some point in the early Middle Ages. Gregory of Tours mentions that a group of "Danes" led by "Chochilaicus" (a possible Latinization of "Hygelac") attacked the Franks around 520 A.D. Little other historical information is written about the Geats.

CHAPTER IV – CHAPTER XV
—

CHAPTER XVI

Frisian–an early medieval tribe of people who occupied parts of what are the modern-day nations of Denmark, the Netherlands, and northern Germany. One of the more advanced societies in the time period known as the "Dark Ages," they traded with silver coins instead of bartering and engaged in maritime trade from the Baltic region to England. They were often rivals of the Franks, who lived to the southwest of their lands.

CHAPTER XVII – XXX

—

CHAPTER XXXI

hides of land–Land in medieval England was measured in "hides." One hide was the amount required to support a family, or approximately 60-120 acres, depending on the quality of the land.

CHAPTER XXXII

—

CHAPTER XXXIII

Hetware–a Frankish tribe that lived near the Rhine River

CHAPTER XXXIV

—

CHAPTER XXXV

Hugas–apparently another name for the Frisians, or a tribe from their lands. Little historical information appears to exist regarding the Hugas, apart from what is written in *Beowulf*.

CHAPTERS XXXVI – XXXIX

—

CHAPTER XL

Franks–the name given to an aggregation of tribes that once inhabited the region of the Roman province of Gaul, the area that is roughly the modern nations of France, Belgium, and parts of western Germany. Much of what we know of the Franks comes from *The History of the Franks*, written by Gregory of Tours, the Bishop of Tours, who lived between 538 and 594 A.D.

Merowings–a tribe of the Franks that eventually came to found the Merovingian dynasty of Frankish kings that began to rule in the early 5th century. Clovis, a Merovingian king who came to power around 486 A.D., united the Frankish tribes and made them subject to his leadership through conquest. He also converted to Catholicism and worked to establish it as the primary religion within his lands.

VOCABULARY

<u>PRELUDE</u>
bedecked – decorated
foundling – an orphan; abandoned infant
hence – "from here;" away
mail – a coat of flexible metal armor, usually comprised of interlocking rings or metal scales
stalwart – brave; hardy, sturdy, strong
tenure – the time period during which one holds an office or position
waxed – grew
wrested – forced from or took by force

<u>CHAPTER I</u>
dire – dreadful, threatening
fens – swamps, marshes, bogs
jubilant – joyful; triumphant
pinnacles – peaks

<u>CHAPTER II</u>
arbiter – a judge
betimes – sometimes, at times
bowers – private rooms in a medieval hall
brook – to tolerate
illustrious – renowned for a position or deed
lament – grief, sorrow
nefariously – evilly, wickedly
parley – a meeting between hostile parties to discuss peace
sore – serious, difficult
sovereign – a king, ruler
thanes – people who hold lands from their lord; liegemen, soldiers
travails – troubles, sorrows, hardships
unremittant – without pause, unceasing
wight – a living being; a creature

<u>CHAPTER III</u>
assuage – to relieve
fain – happily; willingly
fare – journey; move
gainsaid – contradicted; spoke against; contrary to
haven – a safe place; a calm harbor where ships can anchor
headlands – points of land that project into a body of water

marauding – raiding

whence – where

CHAPTER IV

pitched – covered in tar (pitch), waterproofed

scintillating – shining or gleaming brightly

unscathed – unharmed

wends – goes on a course; directs a course

CHAPTER V

boon – a gift, grant, privilege

bucklers – small round shields

helm – a helmet

hither – here

methinks – "I think"

CHAPTER VI

abide – to stay; rest

beneficent – kindly disposed; gracious

bulwark – a defensive wall; a source of strength and protection

fell – evil, dark, dangerous

liegemen – people who have sworn loyalty to a lord; vassals

sagacious – wise; of or relating to a sage; judicious

thither – "to there"

vagrant – a wanderer, especially one who earns subsistence by illegal means

CHAPTER VII

dearth – scarcity; lack (of something)

fealty – an oath of loyalty and service made by a feudal vassal to a lord

CHAPTER VIII

buffeted – hit repeatedly, beaten forcefully

main – the high seas

strove – to have struggled, competed; past tense of *strive*

CHAPTER IX

assailed – attacked

bane – a cause of harm or death

blithe – happy and free from worry

festal – relating to a feast

prowess – power, superior ability

recompense – payment in return, repayment

reprisal – retribution, retaliation
valorous – brave, courageous

CHAPTER X
esquire – the attendant of a warrior or knight
hew – to chop and cut
retinue – a group of servants or attendants, followers
vaunted – boastfully asserted

CHAPTER XI
crags – large boulders
din – a loud and lingering noise (especially one comprised of many various sounds)
ire – hateful anger
sate – satisfy

CHAPTER XII
brandished – waved defiantly (a weapon)
falchion – a broad, curved medieval sword
harrowing – troublesome, tormenting
sinews – muscle fibers

CHAPTER XIII
anon – soon, presently
disparage – to speak ill of; to insult
fallow – not seeded to produce crops; not active
mere – a lake
retainers – household servants
vault – an arched roof; expanse of sky

CHAPTER XIV
baleful – indicating evil; sinister, malicious
reprieve – a temporary suspension of judgment or punishment

CHAPTER XV
ensign – a flag, banner
quaffed – drank
ridden – very full of; driven
sumptuous – rich, lavish, grand
throngs – large crowds, multitudes

CHAPTER XVI
hauberks – breastplates
hillock – a small hill
plighted – to have given a pledge
pyre – a pile of firewood (especially one used for burning dead bodies)
remnants – that which remains

CHAPTER XVII
bereft – robbed or deprived of
diadem – a royal crown
flagons – large vessels, normally made of metal, used to carry and serve wine
lay – an uncomplicated poem; a ballad
magnanimous – generous and noble of spirit

CHAPTER XVIII
bolsters – firm pillows
cuirass – a breastplate; body armor

CHAPTER XIX
barter – to exchange
dauntless – fearless, brave
dolorous – sorrowful, grievous

CHAPTER XX
hart – a deer
heaths – largely desolate areas with scraggly brush for vegetation; vegetation that fills such an area
marches – the border-areas, the perimeter
miscreant – a villain, troublemaker

CHAPTER XXI
drakes – dragons
serpentine – like a snake; twisted

CHAPTER XXII
eddying – swirling, circling
quail – to weaken

CHAPTER XXIII
ardent – passionate, shining, fiery
bandying – exchanging back and forth, as in a game
ephemeral – temporary, passing, transitory
visage – the face

CHAPTER XXIV
aught – nothing
bastion – a fortification, stronghold

CHAPTER XXV
covetous – envious; desiring the possessions of another
nigh – near
overweening – excessively arrogant

CHAPTER XXVI
wielding – waving around; carrying

CHAPTER XXVII
prow – the pointed front of a ship

CHAPTER XXVIII
abject – utterly hopeless, desperate
beseeched – asked earnestly; implored

CHAPTER XXIX
prudence – discretion

CHAPTER XXX
requitals – payment for services

CHAPTER XXXI
barrow – a tomb or vault usually buried beneath a small hill or mound

CHAPTER XXXII
respite – a brief delay or interval

CHAPTER XXXIII
bereaved – in the state of being bereft (see *bereft*)

CHAPTER XXXIV
dirge – a funeral hymn
Elsewhere – death, the afterlife

CHAPTER XXXV
fray – a fight, battle
vanguard – a group or line of troops that advances ahead of others

CHAPTER XXXVI
bequest – a legacy of some sort passed on from one generation to the next
boss – a knob or protuberance at the center of a shield or an ornament
glaive – a spear that has a knife or dagger-sized blade attached to its point

CHAPTER XXXVII
asunder – split apart, separated
winsome – charming, attractive

CHAPTER XXXVIII
cairn – a mound of stones that serves as a marker or memorial

CHAPTER XXXIX
laggards – people who lag behind or move too slowly
wane – to lessen in number or intensity

CHAPTER XL
bounteous – liberal

CHAPTER XLI
ardent – passionate
enmity – severe dislike, hatred
garrison – a fortress armed with troops

CHAPTER XLII
balefire – a bonfire; funeral pyre

CHAPTER XLIII
brands – charred sticks
extol – praise

DANISH ROYAL FAMILY

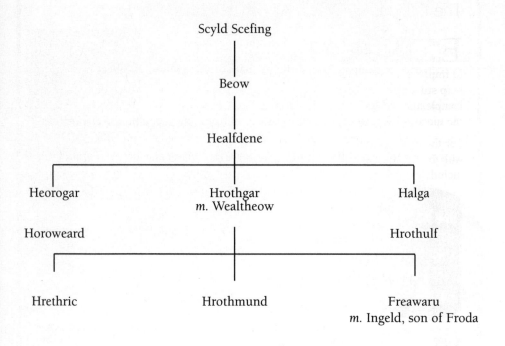

Scyld Scefing

Beow

Healfdene

Heorogar   Hrothgar   Halga
m. Wealtheow

Horoweard   Hrothulf

Hrethric   Hrothmund   Freawaru
m. Ingeld, son of Froda

GEAT ROYAL FAMILY

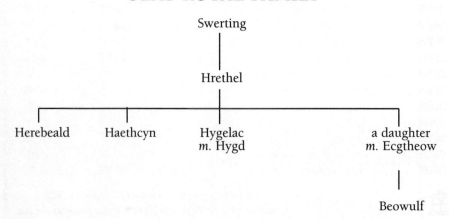

Swerting

Hrethel

Herebeald   Haethcyn   Hygelac   a daughter
m. Hygd   *m.* Ecgtheow

Beowulf

Insightful and Reader-Friendly, Yet Affordable

Prestwick House Literary Touchstone Classic Editions–
The Editions By Which All Others May Be Judged

Every *Prestwick House Literary Touchstone Classic* is enhanced with Reading Pointers for Sharper Insight to improve comprehension and provide insights that will help students recognize key themes, symbols, and plot complexities. In addition, each title includes a Glossary of the more difficult words and concepts.

For the Shakespeare titles, along with the Reading Pointers and Glossary, we include margin notes and various strategies to understanding the language of Shakespeare.

New titles are constantly being added; call or visit our website for current listing.

Special Introductory Educator's Discount – At Least 50% Off

		Retail Price	Intro. Discount
200102	Red Badge of Courage, The	$3.99	$1.99
200163	Romeo and Juliet	$3.99	$1.99
200074	Heart of Darkness	$3.99	$1.99
200079	Narrative of the Life of Frederick Douglass	$3.99	$1.99
200125	Macbeth	$3.99	$1.99
200053	Adventures of Huckleberry Finn, The	$4.99	$2.49
200081	Midsummer Night's Dream, A	$3.99	$1.99
200179	Christmas Carol, A	$3.99	$1.99
200150	Call of the Wild, The	$3.99	$1.99
200190	Dr. Jekyll and Mr. Hyde	$3.99	$1.99
200141	Awakening, The	$3.99	$1.99
200147	Importance of Being Earnest, The	$3.99	$1.99
200166	Ethan Frome	$3.99	$1.99
200146	Julius Caesar	$3.99	$1.99
200095	Othello	$3.99	$1.99
200091	Hamlet	$3.99	$1.99
200231	Taming of the Shrew, The	$3.99	$1.99
200133	Metamorphosis, The	$3.99	$1.99

PRESTWICK HOUSE, INC.
"Everything for the English Classroom!"

Prestwick House, Inc. • P.O. Box 658, Clayton, DE 19938
Phone (800) 932-4593 • Fax (888) 718-9333 • www.prestwickhouse.com

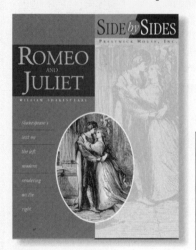